MYSELF & STRANGERS

MYSELF &
STRANGERS

A *Memoir of Apprenticeship*

JOHN GRAVES

Alfred A. Knopf New York 2004

THIS IS A BORZOI BOOK
PUBLISHED BY ALFRED A. KNOPF

Copyright © 2004 by John Graves
All rights reserved under International and Pan-American Copyright
Conventions. Published in the United States by Alfred A. Knopf,
a division of Random House, Inc., New York, and simultaneously
in Canada by Random House of Canada Limited, Toronto.
Distributed by Random House, Inc., New York.
www.aaknopf.com

Knopf, Borzoi Books, and the colophon are
registered trademarks of Random House, Inc.

Grateful acknowledgment is made to Associated Music Publishers, Inc. (BMI) for
permission to reprint excerpts from "Zorongo" from *Canciones Espanolas Antiguas*
Copyright © 1961 by Federico Garcia Lorca—Union Musical Ediciones, S.L.,
Madrid (Espana). International copyright secured. All rights reserved. Reprinted
by permission of Associated Music Publishers, Inc. (BMI).

Library of Congress Cataloging-in-Publication Data
Graves, John, [date]
Myself and strangers : a memoir of apprenticeship / John Graves.—1st ed.
p.   cm.
ISBN 1-4000-4222-4
1. Graves, John, 1920—Childhood and youth.
2. Authors, American—20th century—Biography.
3. Graves, John, 1920—Travel.   4. Americans—Foreign countries.
5. Texas—Biography.   I. Title.
PS3557.R2867Z469 2004
813'.54—dc22   2003058919
[B]

Manufactured in the United States of America

First Edition

To Sam Hynes the instigator,
a cherished staunch friend for more than fifty years

Busquemos la gran alegría del haber hecho.
Let us seek the great happiness of having done.

—Juan Ramón Jiménez, *Máximas*

CONTENTS

Author's Preface   xi

ONE. Origins   3

TWO. A Mexican Interlude   10

THREE. Flounderings, and Escape Across the Waters   19

FOUR. An Island Full of Noises   39

FIVE. Mainly Madrid   95

SIX. Tenerife and Going Home   168

SEVEN. Long Island and the Book   202

EIGHT. The End of a Time   228

AUTHOR'S PREFACE

This memoir is one outgrowth of an old-man's task I set myself to a few years ago, that of putting my papers in order. Reading through my handwritten and sometimes typed journal from the 1940s into the '60s with the intention of burning it afterward, I came to believe that I needed to do more with it. I didn't know exactly why, but the need had something to do with not losing an image of what I once was like, or thought I was like, during an intense period when I was doing a lot of belated apprenticeship floundering in terms of both life and writing.

The memoir touches on some earlier and later swatches of my life, but its main emphasis is on the time between the autumns of 1951 and 1956, including about two and a half years when I was living in Europe, chiefly Spain, and then the time back on this continent that it took me to finish an ill-fated novel begun over there. During none of this period was I in the middle of important things that were happening, whether literary, political, or otherwise. I never have been in the middle of such events except during a brief segment of World War Two, and perhaps during a three-year stint of work for the U.S. Department of the Interior in the late 1960s, in a program whose aim was to "clean up the Potomac River and make it a model for the nation." Nor has being outside of the middle ever bothered me much, or being untypical of any particular group or school of writing.

I did finally consign the old journal to the fireplace flames, but not before excerpting the entries that are preserved here, imbedded in a matrix of retrospective summaries, present-day comments, and square-bracketed explanatory asides. The memoir's form is episodic, in part because the journal was not a meticulously and regularly kept piece of work like a diary. It had many gaps in time and coverage, and certain things of interest, to me at any rate, were skimped or not mentioned at all. I did, for instance, a good bit more fishing in Spain than is indicated here, and especially in the latter part of my stay rode my little green BSA motorcycle to many of the big ferias and fiestas in various parts of the country, with their bullfights, but kept notes on those corridas separately in a pocket notebook that I no longer have. Not that the notes would be of much interest to anyone but me, for they consisted chiefly of private symbols for various cape and muleta passes and other events in the ring. I think I had a fishing notebook too, which has vanished in similar fashion.

Another gap is the near absence of a sense of the natural world and the land, which has been strong in me since childhood and has become even stronger in later life, but which seems to have been somewhat in abeyance during the journal's years. This lack may bother some of my readers, especially those in Texas, where I have been referred to as "The Sage of Glen Rose," a sturdy rustic concerned solely with country things. But I never set out to be a rustic sage, only a writer about things that mattered to me.

Some of the names of people have been changed to avoid offense or injury to those few who may still be living, or to touchy kin of the many who have died.

Here and there the journal or the comments and summaries contain, sometimes verbatim, material I have used in other published work. Such passages had often been lifted from the journal for that other work, or have been borrowed now from the other work for use here. Some have even been altered a little or added to, as memory has furnished more details. I have let all these passages stand, with or without notes regarding their appearance elsewhere.

The journal entries and the comments or summaries often reflect the personalities and views of two different individuals, and have two separate voices. In a few ways Young John the journal keeper is something of a stranger to Old John the gray-headed commentator and summarizer and square-bracketer. He was rather ill-read despite six years of college, naïve in several ways, sexually a bit randy, quite profane at times, and filled with inchoate, often frustrated ambition. And he was still carrying a pretty fair load of ingrained Texan-Southern provincialism. "Callow" may be as good an overall adjective as any to describe him.

But the journal entries convey, as noted above, what he was like back then, or what he thought he was like. And Old John is always there with his eye on his younger self's statements, poised to pounce and criticize when he disagrees strongly.

Many other people's memoirs seem to lead to moral justification of the author's way of life, but I don't seem to have that feeling about my own life, or at any rate about the memoir's particular segment of it. In a short 1960s piece about my attitude toward the Vietnam War, written on request from Gordon Lish at *Esquire* (other writers contributed as well, but the whole politically touchy project was ultimately killed before publication by someone higher up on the magazine's staff), I described myself as "one who has too often glimpsed, skulking from treetrunk to treetrunk behind him, the shadow of his own and his people's imperfection."

I still see that shadow on occasion, and Young John saw it much more frequently. He was, I think, a fairly decent fellow despite his shortcomings, but the chief moral constant I can discern clearly in him is his compulsion to *write,* to write as well as he could, and if possible to write better and better with time. He did stick to that aim, or it stuck to him, and it held him together during a period when demoralization was never very distant.

I considered calling the memoir *The Circle,* for it leads its protagonist from Texas through some other parts of the world, and finally back to Texas again. But the present title, taken at Sam Hynes's suggestion from a sentence of Gertrude Stein's quoted in one of the journal entries, seems to sum it up better.

In a time like ours, I have no notion whether enough people to matter will be interested in a book concerned with the long-past apprenticeship ups and downs of a not especially productive writer like myself, whose main work has been backward-looking, rural, and regional. But it seems I needed to put those ups and downs into words.

John Graves
Glen Rose, Texas
2003

MYSELF & STRANGERS

ONE

Origins

(1920–1945)

I WAS BORN and grew up rather unexceptionally in the prairie city of Fort Worth, Texas, my late childhood and youth coinciding with the years of the Great Depression. My family were "nice people" in the Southern phrase, Episcopalian and conservative, with quite a few of the implicit privileges pertaining to that classification, though my father's struggles to stay financially afloat in the 1930s kept us at times barely within the local Establishment's boundaries.

Lying on the eastern rim of the West Texas ranching country, the city had large stockyards and meat-packing plants, an annual Livestock Exposition with its rodeo, and many visitors who wore high-heeled boots and wide hats legitimately, because these were related to their daily work. But its underlying ethos was also quite Southern. Its mythic heroes were often Confederate soldiers, like my four great-uncles, from both sides of the family, of whom two had gotten themselves killed in battle and a third had lost a leg at Chickamauga. Many of the parents of my contemporaries in the town came from other regions, usually in the South—my own mother was born in South Carolina and my father grew up in coastal Texas with a merchant father, though his mother's people had all been ranchers.

· · ·

Ranching and farming mattered far more in the Texas of those days than they do now. In Fort Worth they were a recent part of most of my friends' family backgrounds, and a number of us, after we were big enough to be of any use, spent our summers doing country work, usually for relatives and at the abysmal rural wages of Depression times. ("A dollar a day and keep" was standard, and workdays often lasted eleven or twelve hours.) My own experience of this sort was not very grand, but it meant a lot to me. One of my older cousins was married to a man who ran a stock farm of several hundred acres not far west of the city, a place that was mainly rangeland, utilized by his beef cattle, and partly creekbottom fields sowed annually to various grain crops.

There I drove an old tractor ahead of a plow, or a binder cutting ripe wheat or oats and tying them into bundles that it dropped into the stubble as it moved along. Afterward I and other workers would stack six or eight of those bundles at a time into shocks to await the arrival of an itinerant thresher, and would do other tasks that needed doing, the most pleasant of which for me—because it had the flavor of old romance—was riding out on horseback and helping to drive in feisty crossbred cattle for branding, dehorning, castration, doctoring, or shipping to market.

There were other fine things about that work. Sometimes I labored alongside talkative Mexican illegals on seasonal jobs like fence repair and firewood cutting, and absorbed from them the Spanish names of things and a stock of unseemly words and phrases. The boss himself, my cousin-in-law, though he was a rough, profane, powerful individual intolerant of weakness in others, was intelligent and had an inquiring mind. He knew much local history, for instance, going back to the Comanche wars of the region, and had a remarkable familiarity with the names and habits of the birds and wild mammals that were all around us there. Later—in part I guess because of him—I went more deeply into these subjects on my own.

And I retained an interest in the land and all that it meant. . . .

. . .

Papa had a well-regarded men's clothing store downtown, but his venerable partner, just before the Depression showed its fangs, had bought a large stock of costly merchandise on credit and had promptly died, leaving Papa with the debt during tough times, in an era when bankruptcy was still a major disgrace. A decent and generous-spirited man, he tried not to impose this situation on his family, but it was there.

Hence, for me, there was a slight element of outsiderness that might have helped to keep me from conforming to the pattern into which most of my Fort Worth crowd fitted comfortably, and might also have helped me to break loose later. There were other such semi-outsiders around, and we tended to know one another and to go our own ways after high school, though a few made the jump and became true Establishment types. People of that more standard ilk most often attended the University of Texas in Austin, joining one of three or four "in" fraternities there and getting to know ruling-class scions from all over the state, with whom they would wheel and deal for the rest of their lives. The friendships I had among them, of which there were enough, were based on having grown up in a neighborhood together and attending the same public schools, and on much hunting, fishing, and other country activity. A number of the less prosperous ones ultimately married money, and as a result made more money and became staid and conservative adults, as their parents had hoped all along they would do. I suppose my parents had hoped for much the same thing, though they never pushed me in that direction.

I was not a rebel loaded with social bitterness, but I did see early that those friends' pattern was not for me. For one thing, I was an inveterate reader and shared few of the ruling passions of their world, such as spectator sports, school spirit, and discussion of what local families had how much money. So when the time came, I attended the small scholarly college of Rice in Houston,

In high school

soaked up literature and history and friendships, and have been grateful ever since for the experience and the institution.

By the time I finished my studies there we had a war on our hands and, along with several million other Americans, I went to it, another break with personal background. Patriotism was involved, of course, but I think mainly I just wanted to see the fighting. If you had grown up on tales of Rebel great-uncles and the Marines at Belleau Wood, you tended to feel that way.

At Quantico, Virginia, I endured candidates' class and was made a second lieutenant in the Marine Corps, got imbued with esprit, went through artillery school, and then was sent to Camp Pendleton on the west coast, where the new Fourth Marine Division was being shaped up. This unit shipped out of San Diego in January of 1944, combat-loaded for the invasion of Kwajalein Atoll.

War is an overwhelming sort of subject and possibly has small pertinence to reminiscences concerned with a writing apprenticeship. But as a force it loomed behind my generation for the rest of our lives, and since my fighting career was pretty short, I might as well summarize it here.

Kwajalein was not a tough battle for most artillerists besides the forward observers landing with the infantry. Our guns were set up on islets within firing range of the main fortified islands, Roi and Namur, which were being pounded by naval gunfire and bombs from aircraft. I and my gun crewmen and our four 75-millimeter howitzers (toys in today's terms) spent the night on one such islet, got sniped at by two or three lingering Japanese who had to be hunted down in the palms and underbrush, and the next morning fired on Roi-Namur in support of the main infantry landing there, until friends and enemies in the beach-head, as reported by our observers on their radios, became so intertangled that we had to stop shooting. And for us that was Kwajalein, though the infantry, as usual, suffered its full quota of casualties.

Then came a sojourn at the new Fourth Division tent camp on a flank of Maui's Haleakala volcano, a pleasant time that didn't last long, for in June we went to Saipan in the Marianas. This was no atoll but a fourteen-mile strip of rough hills full of caves, cliffs, gun emplacements, bunkers, and self-confident hate-filled foemen who gave us hell on the beaches and kept it up as we pushed northward, for the whole time I was there, which turned out to be about two weeks. By then I was on the battalion staff as assistant operations officer, with a section of bright youngsters and duties concerned chiefly with surveying in new gun positions as the infantry advanced and we had to move forward time after time, in order to keep firing in their support. This involved instrument work in a sort of no-man's-land behind the front lines, where bypassed Japanese snipers, most of them fortunately poor shots, could make things interesting on occasion.

The beaches had been rough for just about everybody, but I lost only two men while engaged in that later surveying work, neither of them badly wounded, then received my own comeuppance at battalion headquarters one misty early morning, when

thirty or forty disoriented Japanese, trying I think to get back to
their main force, barged in on us over the top of a little hill and a
brisk firefight ensued. They had the advantage of surprise, but
we had a machine gun and more people and after a time the hill
was quiet. I joined a group going up to check on things, but
when we got among the bodies one turned out to be not a body
but a live Jap playing dead, who—a friend told me later—rolled
a grenade out in front of me which exploded.

The permanent damage turned out to be only the blinding of
my left eye, but that was the end of my career as a combatant.
After a few months in naval hospitals I finished out the war on
limited duty in North Carolina, in charge of a demonstration
battery of howitzers which we fired over recruits arriving from
the Parris Island boot camp. I guess I was lucky, really, not only
in surviving the grenade but in missing out on my division's next
island fight, which was Iwo Jima. On Saipan before I got hit,

Long Beach, 1944

only a few good friends of mine had been killed or maimed, but Iwo took a far bloodier toll.

I didn't feel lucky, though. I felt incomplete. I had been willing, and had gotten pretty good at handling the superb young Marines under my command, and at the work we did with instruments, maps, and guns. But I hadn't managed to last.

TWO

A Mexican Interlude

(1946)

FRESH OUT OF the Marines in late 1945, I spent some time at home in Fort Worth and then went to Mexico. What I had known about that country as a boy in Texas, or had thought I knew, was that it was a very romantic place—a view with sources in my region's literature, in wailed norteño and revolutionary ballads heard on the powerful border radio stations at night, in stints of summertime country work with wetback laborers who had taught me a smattering of their kind of Spanish to back up the classroom kind, in the mere existence of all that colorful foreignness so close to home.

There were even family links of a sort, through my father's mother's people the Cavitts, who had ranched in the South Texas brush country along the Nueces and Frio Rivers. In my time the only surviving relative who knew a lot about this family, having grown up on their ranch, was a warm, bright, old-maid schoolteacher known as Cousin Nora, who for some private reason would not talk about the Cavitts at all. But my father knew quite a few tales that he recounted to me over the years, tales heard from his own mother who had been a child alongside Cousin Nora on that same ranch. These involved not only family eccentricities but Indian raids during which women and children would huddle within a dark house as their men stood on guard outside, forays out of Mexico by the vengeful adherents of colorful, deadly Juan Nepomuceno "Cheno" Cortina, and rustlers and feuds and killings. . . .

One of the stories had been told to Papa not by his mother but his father, who had had no part in it but had tried to help its survivors. And that is the one that fascinated me most when I heard it, and still does.

My grandmother's oldest three brothers had fought in the Civil War and one of them had been killed. The two who came home, one with a peg leg, took up ranching again along the Frio, but within a few years, as the country filled up and the open-range grasses grew skimpier, they moved on west. A younger brother, however, born too late to go to war, remained on the old family land as a rancher. He was known as Monte Cavitt because of his fondness for that card game, and at the age of forty-five he married a Mexican woman much younger than himself, to the disgruntlement of his staunchly Anglo female relatives—I still

Monte Cavitt

have a rather caustic letter one of them wrote about this union. Later family ladies never talked about Monte around me, if for that matter they knew anything, and except for Papa I would not have known his story.

Monte's wife died while bearing their third child and only son, and he kept on ranching and raising his children. The older daughter, even when quite young, was said to be the equal of any vaquero at handling horses and cattle. But a few years after the mother's death, a convicted murderer broke out of jail in one of the region's towns, came to the ranch, killed Monte with an axe, raped this daughter, then about fifteen, and stayed for a few days until an alerted posse rode in and lynched him.

My grandfather went down there from up the coast where he lived, made some sort of arrangements for the children's future, and kept sending money. But the older girl's story tailed off into fog a couple of years later, when she married a man named Navarro, a vaquero by report, and they were thought to have moved to Mexico, though nobody seems to have known for sure. And a part of my fascination with the whole affair has derived from the possibility that I have a few Hispanic cousins down there in northern Mexico or the South Texas brush. . . .

I don't suppose the disastrous tale of Monte Cavitt and his family can be called in any way romantic, but somehow I fitted it in with the Indian and bandit raids and the music and all the rest, and managed to maintain a rosily nostalgic view of our southern neighbors' country up until my own war, nursing it even through the standard grubbiness of tequila-flavored expeditions with college friends to the sin towns across the Rio Grande.

This attitude more or less peaked out for me in the summer of 1940, when I went with a classmate to the timeworn, populous hacienda of his mother's people not far from Linares, riding the last few miles on horseback through rough country with an escort of three armed men. The place had an old stone fortress of a house spraddled around a dusty, busy courtyard, pretty girls—my classmate's cousins, who were home from school and chattered in rapid Spanish that I couldn't follow—vaqueros deft with horses and cattle and rawhide ropes, and, being without electricity, soft lamplight in the evenings. The family's men were called Don This and Don That and some of them wore revolvers against dangers having to do with agrarians, who in the aftermath of revolution and reform had taken over much of the sprawling ranch that in the old days had belonged to Don This's and Don That's and the pretty girls' and my classmate's forebears. It was a tawny nineteenth-century setting straight out of legend, and I'm grateful to have seen it while I still felt as I did then, for that particular sentimentality of viewpoint, along with a few others on varying subjects, seems not to have emerged entirely intact from the war years that followed.

Thus when I headed south of the border again in early 1946, I did so not to seek romance or to immerse myself in learning about the country, but mainly because it was unconnected with my own personal background, and it seemed to be a likely environment wherein to start getting my head straightened out. Such an aspiration, of course, has characterized befuddled young Americans for a couple of hundred years or more, and has usually involved leaving their youthful precincts behind in favor of large cities or foreign lands, where many of them eventually fall into conformity with a new set of values, others are defeated by strangeness and go back home, and a few gain enough clarity of view to carry them on through life and whatever work they have in mind. My own effort of this sort, begun in Mexico in 1946, was to endure sporadically for another ten long years.

It is worth noting that I did not yet think of myself as a writer and indeed wasn't sure I wanted to try to be one, even if that idea was lurking about. What I was chiefly at that point, I suppose, was an inward-looker and a journal keeper, a young man trying

to understand who and what he might be through contemplation of the things that had happened to him thus far, though in
truth not very much had besides an average dose of war.

I went to Mexico City first, where I called Park Benjamin—
an improbable, sometimes ridiculous, and always generous man
in his forties, who weighed around four hundred pounds at that
point. I knew him from my time at Rice in Houston, where I had
been friends with one of his adoptive sons, Homer Buck.

Four hundred pounds are quite a few pounds, of course, more
than anyone's body can carry with ease. But if the reader of these
lines has formed an instant image of Park as a globular figure
with a small head sticking out of its top, he or she has erred. Park
was six feet three inches tall, his large head thatched with dark
curls, his shoulders broad and strong, his manner of walking not
a waddle but a stride which, if it couldn't be described as graceful
with all that weight, carried him confidently up and down stairs,
along sidewalks, and anywhere else he wanted to go. I often
thought he must have been an extremely handsome younger
man, and in fact he was still quite attractive in a way, with regular features, large, expressive, long-lashed brown eyes, a ready
smile, and a frequent, deep-toned, fully genuine laugh.

Park had grown up in social New York and on the Continent,
traveling about with his French-countess mother. The family
was well-connected though devoutly Catholic, and I think he
had cut quite a wide swath in the city when younger. But that
had all ended at some point in the 1920s after a family clash
whose details I never learned, except that it involved his brief
marriage to a chorus girl or cabaret dancer and his renunciation
of the Church, two things that may well have been linked. Most
of his relatives turned against him, one exception being his
favorite cousin Dorothy Park Benjamin, named like himself for
their prosperous grandfather. (A library at Columbia University
was also and I assume still is named for that patriarch.) Dorothy
had married the star opera tenor Enrico Caruso, whom Park had
known and liked. . . .

At any rate, that period had ended with his departure from New York for the Southwest—Arizona at first, I believe—and since then he had functioned usually on the fringes of the oil business. Occasionally he had made a good bit of money and often he had been nearly broke. He spoke four languages perfectly, insofar as I could judge. A huge child in some ways, particularly in terms of money and gourmet food, in the Mexican capital in 1946 he was on a high roll, with a Cadillac and chauffeur, half a floor at the American Club, and influential contacts up and down the Republic. This affluence had resulted from his connection with a tough roofing manufacturer named Suárez, a gallego from the northwestern corner of Spain, for whom Park had been able to obtain cement and asbestos and other needed materials from the United States during the war.

When Park said I was to stay in his apartment, I demurred. "I'm already set up in a good little hotel," I said.

"Nonsense," he said. "You're a friend of Homer's and a friend of mine and you're going to stay here, and that's that."

Things were usually happening when Park was around, and the visit was an interesting one. There was no love lost between him and his gallego benefactor—I don't think there was much love lost between Suárez and any other human being—and with the war finished and normal trade channels open again, Suárez started maneuvering not only to oust Park from his job but to get him expelled permanently from the Republic. Thus in the big apartment in the American Club much telephonic intrigue was in progress. I knew little about its subtleties, but Park saw it as a sort of chess game and loved it. One of his friends, to whom he spoke almost daily, was the head of the Mexican equivalent of the FBI.

Another person to whom he often spoke was his mother in New York, long conversations in French at the end of which there would usually be tears coursing down his broad cheeks. . . .

·   ·   ·

That was a pleasant enough spell, with all there was to see in the capital and on zigzag jaunts in the Cadillac through the surrounding countryside, where Park knew all the local specialties and would stock large glass jars with fiery black-bean tamales and other delights, which we would munch as we rolled along.

None of this was furthering my quest for self, however, if quest it was. I needed to be more alone, and finally told Park this, for he was someone to whom you could tell things.

"Where are you going next, Johnny?" he asked.

"I don't know exactly. Maybe just drift for a while."

"I know a place where you can start out," he said, and two days later he and Ramón the chauffeur drove me to an old run-down hacienda near Altotonga in the highlands of Veracruz state, and left me in the care of its reticent, elderly, impoverished owner, who had no obtrusive desire for intimacy with a gringo. Years later, recollection of that place led me into writing a story called "The Aztec Dog."

My initially lame Spanish, acquired in school and from youthful summertime labor with wetbacks, shaped up fast in those surroundings, for no one in the valley spoke English. I had the use of a good horse while there, and took long rides through the green valley and along the mountainsides, sometimes meeting heavily laden burro trains with attendant arrieros. Their sounds, the clip-clopping of many small hooves on rocky ground or cobbles and the "Arré, burro!" shouts of those who drove them along, are an intimate part of my memory of Mexico back then. Burro trains and the trails they followed were still essential to Mexico's commerce, linking isolated parts of the sierras to their markets, and often, there in the valley or in some small-town inn, I was agreeably aroused from sleep in the early morning by their noise.

The local bigwig, another gallego Spaniard named Pedro Niembro, was friendly because Park had typically grandiose (and typically illusory) plans for turning the old hacienda into a resort hotel and the town into a tourist center. With Don Pedro's son Gregorio, known as Goyo, I went for a stay at their big primitive cattle ranch on a river in the brushy, bandit-ridden tierra caliente below the highlands. Its headquarters was a wide one-story house whose room walls had no ceilings across them, only dark space beneath the high thatched roof, from which scorpions and other creatures would occasionally fall during the night. In the mornings Goyo and I would ride out with the vaqueros, whose main task just then was spotting the numerous screwworm infestations in the ranch's Brahman cattle, expertly roping and throwing the afflicted beasts, digging out the worms with their hands, and filling the hollow wounds with damp clay.

We also visited some sweltering little towns on the coast, one of which strangely was populated by Frenchmen. I have been told that most of that region, including Don Pedro's ranch, is now covered in citrus groves, many of them with French proprietors.

Gallegos like Don Pedro and Park's employer Suárez— natives of the Spanish province of Galicia—seemed to be widely regarded in Latin America as hardnosed and overly acquisitive. In Cuba, the word used to be a hostile designation for all Spaniards. Certainly a good many gallegos did make their fortunes on this side of the Atlantic, but very likely many more stayed and just scratched along. . . .

Some lone-wolf bus-and-train wandering followed Altotonga, for I didn't own a car. I had a portable typewriter and was earnestly pounding out recollections of my life to date, trying to see who and what I was, with heavy emphasis on the war just finished. My participation in the actual fireworks of that conflict, as noted earlier, had been voluntary, rather brief, a bit traumatic, and not at all unusual, but it had also been the most adult and intense experience of my life to date.

One place I remember stopping in during those postwar Mexican months was a guest hacienda near Puebla (or was it Pachuca?) called San Miguel Regla, where cool mountain water had been channeled through a series of pools holding big brown and rainbow trout; this furnished the setting for another of my later short stories, "The Green Fly." Another stop was at "Mi Ranchito" north of Veracruz in the mountains inland from the coast—a little hotel in a green moist valley, with beetles or worms of some sort crunching audibly in the dark beams overhead at night, leaving little sawdust mounds on things below, including my typewriter and clothing and self. No gringos around but me, and that was true of most places I went, so that my Spanish kept on improving. Toward the end of my stay in Mexico some college friends—Buddy Heard, Pat Nicholson, the Brown twins—drove down and met me in the capital and we went to Acapulco, which at that time was a simple and lovely place with a few old-style hotels and not many people. We swam and sunned and drank and talked about our varied experiences in the war, and then we came on home.

Chapultepec, Mexico City, 1946

THREE

Flounderings, and Escape Across the Waters

(1946–1953)

I N THE FALL I went to graduate school at Columbia University on the G.I. Bill. I don't remember much about getting started there, but it had the feel of important things to be learned, and the professors, people like Joseph Wood Krutch and Mark Van Doren and Lionel Trilling, were major figures. Their classes were large lecture affairs, however, so that contact with them was limited.

In December I married my college sweetheart Bryan, who came to New York for the event, to her mother's disgust because we thus avoided a large wedding in Houston. (I think in retrospect that nearly everything about me disgusted her mother, and from her viewpoint she was undoubtedly right.) We lived on East 53rd Street to begin with, then the next summer in a hot top-floor apartment on 110th near Columbia, and the second (and final) year in the basement of a brownstone across from the university on 114th. There were a good many Columbia friends during this time, including most notably Sam and Liz Hynes, and we were part of another group out of Martha Foley's writing class, people disposed toward wildly earnest and argumentative literary parties where much spaghetti and Gallo jug wine were consumed.

Present also in the city were some Texas friends, including my college friend Louis Girard and his Bonnie, he on top of the heap as a young ophthalmologist apprenticed to the New York best and living in luxury at Oyster Bay. And my old college roommate, Jack Staub, was a physician on the battleship *Missouri* at the Brooklyn Navy Yard, paying back the Navy for having subsidized his studies at Duke medical school. Known among friends as the Horrible Doctor or sometimes the Mad Surgeon, Jack was a passionate and precipitate character whose varied obsessions during life, then and later, included coon hounds, birds, bromeliads, and the Ballet Folklórico de México.

Having him nearby was good, and then he turned up Park Benjamin, whom Suárez had finally managed to kick out of Mexico. Park had shrunk down to only three hundred pounds and was dead broke and living on the grudging generosity of well-to-do Establishment relatives, who were all intense Roman Catholics and still angry at him for having left the Church many years before.

Park had the knack of finding small, cheap, excellent restaurants, and I particularly remember one Tuscan place on the Lower East Side, where Bryan and I and Jack would go with him. He had so impressed the owner and the staff with his patrician manner and his deep-voiced rolling Florentine utterances that they would all watch anxiously as the first dish was brought to our table, to see if it pleased him, and would beam when he signaled that it did.

He was living with his mother at her Upper East Side apartment, and when returning to it he would ask the doorman, "Are there any priests or princes up there?" and would go away again if the man smiled and said yes. Yet he told me once that he considered Rome the only true religion, even if it was not for him, and I remember a well-thumbed *Almanach de Gotha* that dominated a small table in his Mexico City living room. He did not seem to have to make sense, Park.

I had the writing bug by then, and was turning out short stories as best I could while coping with study. The first piece I sold was taken, unbelievably, by *The New Yorker,* and a couple of others were published in a short-lived little magazine called *Stateside.* I finished work on a master's degree in English the second year at Columbia, with a thesis on Faulkner, and probably because I wrote pretty well on that document and on examinations, I received a "first" degree, a sort of cum laude designation. I wanted the master's in case I had to make a living as a teacher along my way, but was already fairly sure that true deep scholarship was not my dish—it did not, in me at least, fit well with the writing urge. So I didn't go on into work toward the doctorate.

The following autumn I took a job as a junior English instructor at the University of Texas in Austin. Bryan and I lived in a couple of places while there, the main one being a duplex on Waller Creek in what was then north Austin, just across the street from the little stone-castle studio—a museum by then—of the nineteenth-century sculptress Elisabet Ney, daughter of Napoleon's marshal of that name. Our landlord, who lived with his wife in the other part of the duplex, owned several acres and the creek had sunfish and turtles in it and the big pecans all around held quite a few albino squirrels, whose males the red ones would chase and castrate if they caught them.

A basically miserable, overworked, underpaid period, teaching indifferent freshmen and walking around full of guilt about the ungraded themes sticking out of my coat pockets. I was getting no writing done, nor was our marriage in the best of shape. But there were hunting and fishing along the Colorado from an awkward little skiff I built from a kit, apprentice birdwatching with old Dr. T. P. Harrison the Spenser specialist, and friendships with other instructors, the most lasting of these being with gentle, humorous Lyle Kendall, an eighteenth-century scholar who would also be on the English faculty at TCU in Fort Worth when I taught there in the late 1950s and early '60s, and who later retired to Glen Rose near where I now live, so that we did a lot of visiting and fishing together before he died in 1990.

Bryan and I went to Europe on a Lykes Brothers freighter in the summer of 1949, bicycled and railroaded up and down France with one unsatisfying train trip to Barcelona, had a most pleasant stay in Florence, and came home on a Dutch student ship out of Rotterdam. Not a happy expedition overall, the journal reveals, for I kept selfishly brooding over how much more I could have enjoyed it alone, but instructive and evocative.

Fed up with indifferent freshmen and with other things as well, I took a leave of absence from the teaching job in June of 1950 and never went back. The marriage was crumpling, and I

At the Eiffel Tower, 1949

remember stays at Bryan's family's weekend house at Boerne in the Texas German Hill Country before I finally bailed out. The journal in this stretch is a stew of misery and guilt and thwarted ambition, lasting into the next fall. Bryan was a vital, intelligent, and charming person, but underneath, back then, she had an accumulated load of self-doubt and a tendency toward deep depression that I couldn't cope with at that point in my own life, so at last I walked out because I had to, even though regret dogged me afterward for many years. Still does sometimes, for that matter.

Late in the autumn I went out to Cow Creek valley in the Sangre de Cristo range above Pecos, New Mexico, where I had been before at a small ranch of which my old friend Swede Johnson the Human Cannonball was part-owner. (He had a trick, not viewed with pleasure by the owners of honkytonks, of charging down the length of a barroom and running up the wall at the far end, kicking the ceiling, then flipping backward to the floor on his feet.) By then the big Swede, married and a father, was doing well in the mortgage-and-loan business in Albuquerque.

We had met while having our butts paddled as pledges to one of the silly little high school fraternities of the prewar era, and we had recognized the silliness and laughed about it with each other, though we endured the trials of pledgehood for the privileges, mainly Christmas dances, that membership conferred. Friends from then on, we had kept up with each other sporadically ever since, even while attending different colleges and during the war, when I was in the Pacific and he was navigating a B-17 over Europe.

The little ranch, with a comfortable lodge and a clear, cold creek, was an idyllic spot, but its wino caretaker, a sweet old fellow, was chummy and garrulous and did not view my typewriter-pounding as serious enough work to hinder his loquacious visits to my room. So quite soon I moved two or three miles downstream on the creek to a one-room log house rented from a Mexican rancher. The place had no electricity and few amenities beyond a wood-burning cookstove, some utensils, a lantern, a cot, a bucket for bringing water up from the creek, and a separate privy. But it served. I even took fairly regular baths, sloshing warmed water on myself from a chipped enamel dishpan.

I was writing furiously on faulty short fiction, and in the beginning left the valley only to go to Pecos for groceries and to use a laundromat, driving every few days up and over the hump through slushy snow, with chains on the tires, to the store-and-bar where they had a psychotic Doberman with his teeth worn to round stubs from fetching rocks the loafers threw for him. Swede came up from Albuquerque when he could, and before winter really set in we hunted doves a few times in the desert brush below Pecos, walking them out of the mesquite trees and then later, in the cool of evening, waiting for them by a water hole.

As spring started edging slowly in, flowers blossomed in the valley's fields, and I started going for groceries to Santa Fe, where Swede would sometimes drive up to meet me in some bar. We sat and talked and sipped and watched the arties and ranchers and pseudo-ranchers and sunbrowned Eastern divorcées. It was an easier-going town back then than it is now.

I would wander often along trails on the mountainside above my cabin and on one stroll met a black bear, who studied me for a while before wheezing and loping off. And once I rode horseback with my landlord's seventeen-year-old son up into the national forest, to check on the fifteen or so cows for which they had grazing permits. We were counting on little trout from the rivulets for sustenance and thus took along only cornmeal and lard and salt. But it turned cold and the trout hid themselves and what we ate instead was a porcupine, very stringy provender tasting of spruce bark, and two blessedly stupid blue grouse that Jesusito was able to kill with thrown sticks. There was plenty of cornpone, though.

With Swede or alone, I did a lot of trout fishing up and down the creek as it warmed, wading in tennis shoes and making stealthy short casts among the streamside alders with a light seven-foot rod and tiny nymphs and dry flies I tied myself. These were small brook trout and rainbows—twelve inches was a big one—but their delicate pursuit gave me just as much pleasure as the larger fish I sometimes sought over on the Rio Grande in its gorge above Santa Fe.

I stayed in the cabin till June, when big Swede ran his car into a deep ravine near Galisteo one Friday night, while driving up to fish with me, dying on Saturday in a Santa Fe hospital after I got down there to see him and gave some blood. The surgeons had done what they could for him, but in those days and that place they couldn't do much, with his crushed chest and severed spinal cord.

"You'll be doing the Human Cannonball again before long."

His face was puffy and bruised and his eyes were closed, but the corners of his mouth lifted in suggestion of a smile. "Tell you . . . something," he whispered.

"What?"

"Don't ever . . . cannonball a God-damn canyon . . . Doesn't work."

He had been a close, alive, sometimes troublesome friend, and after that I was finished with New Mexico.

I spent several weeks that summer with Sam and Liz Hynes, my friends from Columbia University, in their rented house on the eastern shore of Mobile Bay. He was a Minnesotan who had been a Marine pilot during the war (about which experience he later wrote a strong book called *Flights of Passage,* a cult item to this day among old fliers, and some not so old), and by then was teaching at Swarthmore. Liz was from Alabama and for years they spent their vacations there on the shimmering bay in a pleasant, hot, sleepy town called Fairhope, quite Southern but with the difference that it had been founded by Midwestern disciples of single-tax economist Henry George. We wandered along the shore talking literature and philosophy, nosed through the rubble at old Fort Morgan whose torpedoes Farragut had damned, netted crabs, and went fishing with locals in little tea-brown, sand-bottomed pinewoods rivers, catching smallish largemouth bass that they called "green trout."

The wide bay in summer had a periodic though unpredictable occurrence called a fish jubilee, when aquatic creatures of a number of species would throng together in great squirming heaps in the shallows near shore, usually at night. When the word got around, locals would start thronging too, leading rowboats out and pitchforking them full of sea trout, stingrays, redfish, crabs, eels, and God knew what else. It was quite a sight to watch. Probably there is an explanation of this phenomenon by now, but if so I've never seen it, though a knowledgeable type did once tell me that there was just one other place in the world where it happened, a bay somewhere on the coast of India.

Afterward, in September, I had a brief and doomed reunion with Bryan in Houston. The father of a friend of ours, a blunt man who liked us both, told me finally, "John, you've got to shit or else get off the pot!"

Guiltily, I chose to do the latter, going to New York and taking a timeworn one-room apartment on East 15th Street between Union Square and Irving Place. It had a closet kitchen, a tiny bath, a Murphy bed that folded down from the wall, and two windows opening onto a wide airshaft from which at night, in those unairconditioned times, there came to my ears the sounds of human grief and laughter and rage and lust, and the squalling of cats. But it was cheap, and it had a small table just the right height for my Smith Corona.

Still the desperately aspirant writer and still full of shame over the marital fiasco, I wrote and wrote and wrote doggedly on fiction, some of it bad and some a bit better if only in aim, and a few pieces, mainly bad, were sold and published. During this time I was writing "one for them and one for me," which meant one dishonest silly story, aimed at the slick magazines and their money, for each of my own serious efforts. A handful of the slick ones sold, while "mine" were predominantly failures, even in my own eyes. . . . There was clearly a lot of apprenticeship still ahead, even at age thirty-one.

The slick magazines were still in their glory then, though not much farther down the road they would be shouldered aside by television, which took over their clutch on the market for middle-class affirmation. The best-known and best-paying ones like *Collier's* and *The Saturday Evening Post* (to which I never managed to sell anything) had published a few excellent authors including Faulkner and Fitzgerald, though seldom their best work. And there were many imitators which paid two, three, even five hundred dollars for a piece of sentimental or fake-comic guff, at a time when dollars went much further than they do now. Most of my published efforts in that world, done under a pseudonym, are fortunately not of record, but the money helped.

I got enough things into print to think about finding an agent, for I knew I wouldn't be staying for long in the city to do my own dealing with magazines. A friendly editor, Eleanor Stierhem, made a short list for me of agents she thought might suit me and be suited by me, and I started down it, undergoing interviews and submitting samples of my work. The first one I tried didn't care for what I showed him, the second I didn't care for personally, and the third was John Schaffner, a gentle, civilized, not very commercial-minded man of good taste, married to the daughter of the poet Hilda Doolittle. He handled my writing with understanding and acumen for thirty-odd years after that, not making nearly enough money out of his ten-percent cuts to justify his efforts.

There were a couple of women along the way, encounters rather than relationships, for I was being wary of entanglements just then and for a good while afterward. Became a regular at Pete's Tavern on Irving Place near where I lived, run by old Peter Belles who remembered waiting on O. Henry there ("Mr. Porter") when he had been young and just out of Italy. I came to know the random crowd who hung out in Pete's, some of them young doctors and scientists from the nearby NYU medical center, some lace-curtain Irish alcoholics, a few from the fringes of what was then called café society (I remember one slightly faded beauty whose claim to fame was having been one of Elliott Roosevelt's girlfriends), and a sprinkling of heterogeneous types like me. That bar, incidentally, was the only place on earth where I have ever been known as "Tex," a sobriquet bestowed by Pete himself, who managed to give even that monosyllable a strong Calabrian accent.

There were real friends, too—Jim Derryberry from the Marines, prospering in advertising and living in style in an eighteenth-floor apartment on Beekman Place where I would sometimes spend weekends when feeling too grubby on 15th Street; brilliant and arrogant Abe Rothberg from the Columbia days, then teaching at Hofstra College on Long Island; the girls from Fort Worth with their jobs at magazines and their apartment on East 63rd Street where visiting or resident Texans often assembled. Jack Staub had left by then, out of the Navy and doing his surgical residency in Houston, and Park Benjamin had somehow escaped dependence on his relatives and gone back to Texas too, but Louis Girard, M.D., and his Bonnie were still out at Oyster Bay, living well and having access to a comfortable ketch in which I cruised with them two or three times on Long Island Sound.

Not that I saw these people all that often; mainly I was alone at the typewriter, spending the evenings at Pete's or walking west a few blocks, perhaps with a friend, to visit Greenwich Village gathering places like the San Remo, where you could watch ragged old Joe Gould perform his elbow-flapping, squawking seagull act for drinks, talk Spanish with a Valencian waiter who had fought on the losing side of that Civil War, or rub elbows with the hard-drinking, liberal-literary elite of those times, chiefly transmuted hinterlanders. These were heirs to a version of the hard-core leftism of the thirties that had been watered down by (1) postwar awareness of Stalinist brutality and duplicity, and (2) the menace of rampant McCarthyism, very much alive at the time.

I envied this group their certainties about what was right and what wrong, which I was far from sharing. If one was inclined toward thought, a Southern background made pat answers come hard, and as I have noted, the Texas of my youth was quite Southern. By now I had sidled out from under many of the harsh or sentimental dogmas of that heritage, but I had never worked up a set of easy attitudes, whether rightist or leftist in flavor, through which to pass pat judgment on people and events. For that matter, I still have not.

Or was Southernness the reason for this? My Columbia friend Abe Rothberg, whose Jewish political heritage came straight from the old left, had thought his way through all of that to a point close enough to mine that we could, while frequently disagreeing, like and respect each other and communicate on just about all subjects. The easy-answer people, at the San Remo and the White Horse Tavern and around, Abe called "gliberals. . . ."

They were not my kind of folks and New York was not my kind of town and I knew it. But at a time when I needed badly to be unfettered and alone most of the time with my writing, the city served my purposes well.

It was also a gentler place back then. Sleepless and pondering some tough paragraph or other problem, you could go out and walk the empty streets after midnight with no apprehension at all.

In early December of 1952 I went home and then to California to visit my friend Homer Buck, who had been called back to duty for the Korean War as a Marine helicopter pilot. He was living with three or four other unmarried pilots in a rented house at Corona del Mar, and being there was a bit like returning to my own wartime days, with the drinking and the usually bootless barroom pursuit of girls and all that. Homer and I also poked around in tidepools along the coast (he was a biologist and later took his doctorate in fisheries management), and once we went down to Ensenada and caught a tow sack full of colorful species off of a party boat. Home to Texas again with him for Christmas, hitchhiking on a very battered B-17 returning from Korea for repairs.

Homer, as I have noted, was one of Park Benjamin's boys. Park did have some ridiculous qualities, but he was also a kind and generous man, and during his twenty years or so of living in the Southwest he had always kept an eye out for promising kids in need of help.

The first ones he found were in Arizona: young Homer and his older brother Willard, who at thirteen or fourteen had been supporting the two of them through manual labor—in a copper mine, I think—after their parents, small farmers, had both died. Park took them in and raised them, mainly in Houston where I first knew him and them. And along the way he found five or six others to take in and help. All got good educations—subsidized by Park when he was flush, or by contributions from older members of the pack when he wasn't—and ended up in professions ranging from nuclear physics to veterinary medicine and banking.

In our convoluted age, I guess, some people while reading the last two paragraphs will have said to themselves, "Aha, gay hanky-panky!" But I knew all of those boys, some well and others slightly, and nothing of that sort had ever touched them. Park's sexuality, Staub the Mad Surgeon and I once decided, had at some point been shunted away from women into food. His eyes would glisten when a table was being served, and his hands would toy with knife and fork.

At any rate, when Park in Houston heard from Homer that I was heading for Europe in January of 1953, he called me in Fort Worth and in effect demanded (I guess I was more or less one of his boys too by then) that I take along his latest protégé, an eighteen-year-old Mexican named Ángel Sánchez, whose viewpoint he wanted broadened. I had known the boy when down there in 1946 and had liked him. Park had found him after his Spanish father had died; he was leading a street gang, but had piled up an impressive record during a two-year scholarship at a private school, and had kept it up when Park had sent him back there. So I agreed to see Ángel through a little of France and more of Spain, from whence he would go on to Italy and I to the Balearic Islands.

My father's reaction when I told him I was going to Europe was typical, and may show why I remained as fond of him as I did. I knew I had been a disappointment to him in a number of ways—not wanting to take over the store as a merchant, quitting teaching and a wife whom he liked very much, leading, as far as he knew, a bohemian existence in New York. . . .

Therefore at this point I expected something of a blast, and I wouldn't have blamed him for it.

But what he said, with a smile, was, "What are you going to do when you find out you don't like it over there?"

He was wrong, because I did like it over there and the sojourn did me much good in the long run. But I realized anew how glad I was to have him as a parent.

Ángel and I embarked from New York in late January on the

brand-new SS *United States,* in tourist class because I was under Park's injunction to hold expenses down while with the boy, not that I myself could have afforded much better. I had a brief, intense, adulterous romance on board the ship with a superb if discontented woman, the wife of an American officer in Germany. Ángel and I sightsaw in Paris a little and went to Spain, and I split with him, as planned, in Barcelona in late February.

The following are journal entries from that trip:

FEB. 13, MADRID: And so day before yesterday away from Paris, a cold damp place at this season, with an atmosphere (worse than last time) of screwing strangers. We took a luxe third-class train via the Loire to Tours, then down through rich French countryside—Angoulême, etc.—to Hendaye. Many mixed thoughts which I have forgotten. So easy to see why Frenchmen antiwar; they want no more. Have things all worked out. We with the neurosis of progress want everyone else neurotic too. Usual change in people in our compartment from north to south, from silent tight-lipped to voluble. Bearded nervous poet type, wife, child, and poodle. Friendly old farmer at Bordeaux, going home. His prescription for living long: good wine, eaux chaudes. Rattling French of the south, hard to understand. He was polite but unhappy about 20,000 American soldiers stationed near Bordeaux. Me, too. What are we doing there, getting drunk and chasing their women? All military are thus, why not keep them at home where people can get mad at them because they're soldiers, not because they're of some specific nationality.

Recent reading: Robert Graves, *The White Goddess* (not yet through). Jesus, what a combination of scholarship with feeling. He may be off track—I don't think too much—but if so he is nevertheless demonstrating a beautiful mind of a type America is not likely to produce. Inferiority complex? No, but they have it on us there—Greek & Latin in the cradle, etc. What I have to do is define American-ness, develop it in me. Hemingway did, but I don't want it the same way. Waugh, *Scoop,* usual cruel delightfulness of man from older quieter world confronted with one aspect or another of modernity—here journalism and imperialist politics. Waugh, *When the Going Was Good* (not finished)—creates envy of those traveling days, also of the English setup where someone from your public school turns up at a crossroads in Kenya Colony, and you have friends everywhere. Boy, how they had themselves fixed up. Of course even in that setup I'd probably have been a lone wolf. Can't say I think too much of his choice of places to visit, but he explains. In those days you couldn't see the old world breaking up (but he *did,* in his novels), so it is not worth study. Frank Harris, *My Life and Loves.* Completely egocentric old man bragging. Couldn't read the absurd literary parts, sought the prurient passages. "I, I, I!" Mental masturbation about things he never did. Or if he did he should have been kicked in the butt. "Beauty contest" at villa, all crap. Peculiar prudishness, despite his pornographic intention, that prevents him from going all the way and using the right words for male and female organs. Fatuous old liplicker, sadist, probably queer. Any ordinary husband has more useful knowledge of the sexual act.

FEB. 15: With a bad cold. Young Falangists or somebody singing outside the hotel all morning in the street. Still singing. I don't know who they are but their artificial enthusiasm and their clear sense of youthful importance irk me.

Ángel comes in and reports that they are conscripts. That somehow makes them less offensive, village boys bound for the Army without recourse.

Knowing no French, Ángel had been rather lost and subdued in Paris and had stuck pretty close to me as we explored museums and palaces and parks. But in his father's country, after we had crossed the border at Hendaye and taken a Spanish train, he came alive, chatting with strangers and disappearing for hours on end to study the local scene by himself.

He was a fiery little democratic liberal. On the train trip to Madrid, a lordly bishop in purple and gold came into the dining car where we were seated and was greeted with servility by its staff. Ángel viewed this with shock and indignation, and I had to shush him at one point. In Mexico during his whole lifetime and for years before, priests had had to hide or remain unobtrusive, and he had grown up enthusiastically anticlerical.

We had become close during the trip and I was very fond of him, but he was an intense and talkative companion for a loner like me, and by the time we had "seen Madrid" and had taken another train to Andalucía in southern Spain I had started craving solitude again, as indicated in the following entry:

FEB. 19, SEVILLA: This is a great problem for you—the matter of loneliness vs. the ennui of being too much with someone. Only special people can I be with for long without resenting their intrusions—they have to be independent like me, taking off when they feel like it, meeting up again, all casual. How will you ever manage marriage? With money, maybe. What I'm going to have to attain is the old British ideal of the traveling scholar: books etc., being alone and not minding—but without retreating into the impossibility of communication, rather standing ready to talk, to know, to do things with people. It can be done, and I am much closer to it now than I've ever been.

Winding toward the end of Graves's *Goddess,* lost often in alphabets and mythologies. Beautiful, nevertheless, and his ultimate round-eyed admission that it's all the rationalization of a hunch—a.k.a. poetic intuition—is fascinating. Enormous learning, etc., then the simple arrogant British statement that he had just believed these things. I can't go all the way with him on all the ideas, among those I understand—e.g., that in a matrilineal goddess society women are the rapists, etc., but so much of it is fine and wholly believable. It will stand— require—rereading. I hope I can get a number of books in Barcelona. Should have brought more but too damn bulky and heavy.

FEB. 25, GRANADA: The recurrent looking-out-the-train-window feeling of what am I doing here, why not marriage, somehow content, warm same bed at night, children . . . This is then ameliorated by the knowledge that I have at least made a vain stab at that, and by pleasurable anticipation of the life yet to come. I can work it all out if I stay watchful.

The Robert Graves book second-thoughted with odd dissat-isfaction. Wonderful demonstration of intelligence, and a godawful lot of needs-to-be-said truth, but so much in the end proves to be a rationalization of things to fit his system. Good system, works for him, but like Catholicism, I can't take it whole. Am always hoping someone will present me with a system. Will have to work one out for myself, but much of it will come from other people's systems, like this one, like Yeats's. Glad to have read the Graves, will reread, even though I am convinced that much of the alphabet stuff is like *Finnegans Wake,* complication for complication's sake.

In Sevilla we had viewed the things one is supposed to view— the ancient Alcázar fortress remodeled long before into a palace, the cathedral with its Giralda spire that had once been part of a mosque, the ornate bullring, gypsy flamenco dancers—and like many thousands of foreign visitors before us had tried out the pretty fallen fruit from orange trees in the parks, only to find them immensely sour and fit only (and especially) for making marmalade. And at Granada we kept on being touristic, with primary attention to the Alhambra. From there we took a slow bus eastward on winding roads through high, arid land with sunbaked towns that looked to have been asleep since the Moors had been driven out of them.

It was a good trip, though, in part because on the bus I met another American, an intelligent young fellow named Pryor, just back from combat in Korea and wandering around Europe alone in an effort to reconstruct his civilian self, as I had done in Mexico after my own war, and was perhaps still doing to some extent. He and I talked and talked about war and many other topics, both of us loquacious from a period of speaking little English, and we were friends by the time the bus descended into a lush semitropical valley and arrived at the city of Murcia, which billed itself as "the Rose of Spain" but was in fact, at that time, a sad and shabby provincial sort of place. The three of us spent the night in a dumpy hotel room, taking a horse cab in the morning to the railroad station and a train to Valencia, on which Pryor and I continued our conversation while Ángel, a bit disgruntled by his linguistic exclusion, studied the passing fields and hills.

Pryor was the first questing war veteran I had run into on this trip, though I had known many of them in graduate school at Columbia in the forties and would know others, some not American, during my stay in Europe. This young man was not from my war, but it didn't matter. We knew things together because we had both been there.

More sightseeing in Valencia, some fine seafood at the long beach called the Grao, then farewell to my new friend and with Ángel another train trip, north into Cataluña.

FEB. 25, BARCELONA: Ángel came in just now with a story that was rather nice. He found a young pretty prostitute in a café, talked to her and bought her a drink. They discussed the hatefulness of priests, among other things, and got friendly. He told her frankly that he was broke and couldn't go with her [the money that Park was to send him in Barcelona had not yet come], and she said hell, we'll go anyhow. They did, all for love, and afterward she bought him a pack of cigarettes. Her farewell: "Ay, majo, qué poco dura lo bueno!" How brief the good times are. . . .

FEB. 28, SAME: *Brideshead Revisited* revisited for about the third time—nice still, though it's funny how his talent wobbles sometimes when he's being serious—can be corny about a woman's beauty, for instance. When Anthony Blanche is telling the protagonist Charles Ryder about the defects of his painting—charm, etc.—I think it is Waugh talking to himself.

Ángel finally received his remittance, and I saw him off on his jaunt to the Riviera and Italy. I found myself relieved to be again alone, even knowing that loneliness would ensue, as it always did. I changed to a somewhat more expensive hotel where I could rest with more ease and didn't have to cope with the heavy "American Plan" food of the one in which we had been staying.

Eleanor Stierhem, my New York editor friend, had given me the names of a few people to look up in Spain. I hadn't used any of these before now, but with two or three days on my hands before a boat would leave for Mallorca, I called a married American couple on her list who lived in Barcelona, and was invited to lunch.

This meal with Professor and Mrs. Walter Kuhn was instructive though not a complete delight. The professor, a portly man in his middle or late sixties, had Harvard connections and was an accepted authority on Catalan art, which he spoke of interestingly and with deep knowledge. On other subjects, however, he tended to be dull or sometimes dogmatic and irksome, particularly in regard to politics.

I have remarked on my own ambivalence toward such matters, and have usually been able to get along all right with widely divergent political thinkers as long as they are not vociferously extreme, whether on the left or the right. And Walter Kuhn, Ph.D., was pretty extreme, an avid Franco partisan who had "seen all" in a few days in Barcelona in 1936, before making his homeward escape.

"The Reds were animals," he said. "Complete animals. They looted and vandalized the churches and killed priests and nuns and anyone else whose looks they didn't care for."

And so on.

I had read and thought enough about the Spanish Civil War to know that most of what he said was true, but I knew also that the Nationalists, Franco's people, had been just as savage wherever they had controlled a Republican region. Hot hatred flowing in both directions had been the main villain in that complex, fratricidal bloodiness.

I kept my mouth shut, though, having no axe to grind.

The professor's much younger wife Jan Kuhn, fiftyish and still pretty, had probably, I surmised, once been a student of his. She clearly did not differ with his views, but was friendly and gracious, and helpful regarding Mallorca, where they spent the summers. According to her, everything was fine there; you could live well and cheaply. It sounded good.

The Spanish Civil War, which had ended only fourteen years before that luncheon, after wiping out several hundreds of thousands of persons, would be a thematic awareness, usually subsurface but always present, during the whole of my stay in that nation.

FOUR

An Island Full of Noises

(1953)

I HAD PROBABLY chosen Mallorca as an alighting-place because of talks with Martha Foley at Columbia and during my later New York sojourn. In the 1930s she and her then husband Whit Burnett, while living on the island, had started *Story* magazine, whose promotion of honest short fiction in English caused it rather rapidly to become quite successful, at least in terms of the "little magazines" of the time. Mallorca under the Spanish Republic, though its period of rampant tourism was still in the distant future, had evidently been a minor center for American and British esthetes, writers, and painters. Martha liked to recount their names, of which I recognized only a few. Robert Graves had been the most prominent—still was in my own day, having returned after the Spanish Civil War and World War Two—but she had never met him, for in British fashion he had stayed remote from the rest of the foreigners as he did even now, living in the purely native hill town of Deyá.

So in early March of 1953 I took a ship from Barcelona to Palma, a city I still envision as creamy gold in color, the tint of the stone in its cathedral, in the small Bellver Castle on a mountainside, and in many of its other buildings. I stayed there—not counting a side trip to Pamplona and the Pyrenees, and another to the Riviera, Italy, and Switzerland—until the following November. My journal during those months was more voluminous than elsewhere, for I was doing less writing than I had intended to do, and the literary compulsion often diverted itself into scrawled journal entries, a boring number of which were devoted to complaints about that very unproductiveness.

Many entries also were concerned with the people I came to know in Palma. At first these were chiefly members of the expatriate crowd, of whom only a sprinkling bore any resemblance to the artistic and literary types of the early 1930s, at least as those had been described to me by Martha. The predominant specimens now were hard-drinking idlers—Establishment Americans and assorted similar natives of Canada, Scandinavia, Holland, and other prosperous regions, with some British and French who tended to stay within their own groups. Only a few of these people spoke much Spanish or took any interest in the local scene. Most were living high in the upper-class bayshore suburbs of El Terreno and C'as Catalá that stretched west from the old city center, for Spain was very cheap in those days if you had access to a little foreign currency. Some of these gentry had family money that upheld their style of life, while others were living on savings from earned income, or whatever. I myself had a small military pension and irregular payments for pieces of my writing sold by John Schaffner in New York.

This crowd drank and partied more or less constantly, and in the beginning I drank and partied quite a bit with them and even had brief episodes with a couple of the women. However, I hadn't come to Spain to lead that sort of life, but with the aim of clarifying my view of who I was and what I had come out of, and of getting my writing in order. On the island, therefore, I kept pulling away from involvement with the expatriates, and in the long run my most meaningful relationships were those I had with local people.

The writing I was doing when I arrived there was still "one for them and one for me," but after a while I began to feel queasy about the cheap pseudonymous fiction and finally started back-

ing away from it, though most of the "ones for me," the more
serious efforts, continued to be principally apprenticeship stuff
up to and including the novel I began writing in the Canaries
toward the end of my stay abroad. But there were some encour-
agements along the way also, including the fact that a couple of
short stories mentioned in the journal ended up in one or
another of the annual "best" collections back home. One of these
crops up in the following passage, the first journal entry of my
Mallorcan sojourn:

MARCH 5, PALMA: Second day here after a boat ride, regis-
tration in a dull Class 1A hotel. Called Mrs. Kuhn's friends the
Jordans and am to go there to dinner tomorrow evening, but
meanwhile am just frankly thrashing. Worse than that, have
hit one of these temporary spells where I know no one, find
communication overwhelmingly difficult, and all the people I
see are paired and bunched off. Ironically these times are when
I most want communication.

Of course, Schaffner's news about "The Green Fly" being
accepted by *Town and Country,* coming the day I left Barcelona,
helped some, though not as much as might have been expected.
I know I am committed to writing by now, and I don't need a
further external excuse. But that is the first *real* story out of my
recent writing that has been accepted. It won't be the last. The
accomplishment from now on is not to be selling, but writing
them. They'll sell, enough of them.

The couple to whom Jan Kuhn had sent me, Jim and Sarah
Jordan, occupied a rather gloomy pile of gray granite, staffed with
five servants, on the bay in the C'as Catalá suburb. Their prosperity was Midwestern in derivation—automotive I believe—but
Jim had attended a Connecticut prep school and Yale, and their
outlook and prejudices were those of the upper East Coast elite.
They were quite hospitable when I showed up for dinner, which

was served after a quantity of strong waters had been consumed. In time a friendship developed between us, with reservations on both sides—theirs because they did not quite know what to make of a fellow who was reasonably literate and well-mannered but a Texan nonetheless, and mine because of the precarious brittleness of their relationship, which became apparent after a few drinks taken when their usual excessive endearments—"dear," "sweet," "darling," "pet"—would develop a sardonic edge.

Others present that evening included a fortyish couple named Allingham, Dick and Carol, he also a Yalie though a pretty sodden one, and she, as I found out later, the intelligent and perceptive offshoot of a prominent family of Jewish financiers in New York, once beautiful but now gaunt from bungled back surgery, and usually somewhat sozzled. Rounding out the table were plump, pretty Marie Colton, a multilingual young local woman of mixed British and French parentage, and Robert Cochrane, a large, charmingly humorous, sandy-haired urban character who was a little younger than myself.

During the coming weeks I would come to know all of these people and others much like them quite well, and often to learn more about them than I really wanted to know. In large part this was because another of Jan Kuhn's favors had been a recommendation that I rent the smaller villa next door to the Jordans till mid-May, when she and her professor husband, who leased it each summer, would come out to Palma from Barcelona and take it over. The little stuccoed building, with its tiled roof terrace overlooking the bay, seemed fine to me and I moved in. Its rent was only about $45 a month and included a likable, gossipy young maidservant named Margarita, whose sister and brother worked for the Jordans. But being there put me squarely within the expatriates' zone of social ferment for the next two months, a situation I would come to regret.

Meanwhile, though, I settled in, installing my typewriter on a small table on the terrace and pecking away there during a series of calm, clear, warm days. In the evenings Margarita fixed my supper before going home, and if I wanted company I could find it next door, for the Jordans remained friendly.

This agreeable pattern could not last, however. One day, bored with what I was writing ("one for them") and wanting to see more of the island, I rented a motorbike and took a long ride along the ruggedly beautiful north coast. On the return trip a wet cold front slammed in, and by the time I got home I was soaked and chilled and within two days was miserably down with fever and a chest condition that was possibly pneumonia. I dosed myself with Terramycin tablets given to me by Jack Staub the Horrible Doctor before I had left Texas, downed the soups and teas that Margarita prepared, clucking with sympathy as she served them, and finally emerged on the other side of the crud—soured, lonely, and devoid of ambition.

Then there was Simone. . . .

On the afternoon when I met this lady, I was three days out of bed and still weak. Walking a few blocks toward downtown Palma, I picked up a spy novel at a little British lending library, and on my way home stopped in briefly at a place labeled Joe's Bar on a little square called the Plaza Gomila, where there was a talkative group of seemingly pleasant and interesting Americans and other foreigners, and I was utterly and entirely and obviously alone and outside of things.

One man said to a good-looking brunette, "Where did he find a ladder?"

She laughed. "I don't know, but it didn't do him any good. He couldn't get his big belly through the window."

The sense of exclusion on arrival in new places was not unfamiliar to me; it was much as I remembered first visits to Pete's Tavern in New York. I knew it would pass, but feeling as shaky as I did just then it made me see myself as inadequate, timid, and dull as I sipped brandy and thumbed through my book at the bar. I left, and instead of going home took a trolley a long way west as it ran parallel to the shore, separated from it by limestone and granite and stucco villas. I was still feeling very much alone, and when the trolley line and the villas ended I walked on in late afternoon to a section of gray rocky shore with sandy patches, above which a black Citroën was parked among scrub pines. There I sat down on a boulder and took out my book.

But just then a tallish young woman in red slacks and espadrilles showed up in a hurry from behind a point. She angled behind me toward the Citroën, but I heard her stop.

"Óigame, por favor," she said. Listen, please.

To my ear the intonation was not Spanish, and when I looked around I knew I was right, for Spanish women did not carry breasts like those around under only a halter, in public. She had dark, parted hair held back by a kerchief, and was quite pleasant to look at, perhaps nearing thirty.

"Sí?" I said.

"I just hit a man with a rock!"

It sounded like a threat, with throaty French r's, and I started laughing. "Where?" I asked.

"In the stomach," she said. "Or lower down. He was . . . how? Exhibitioniste."

"Good," I said. "But I meant, where did you do it?"

"There he is!" she said, pointing, and fifty yards away, a little beyond the point's rock jumble, a man with tousled hair and a dirty shirt stopped, scowling at us.

The girl waved a fist and cursed him in French, whereupon he shook his own fist at us, shouted something, then turned and disappeared.

"I'm glad you were here," she said.

"Me, too."

"You're not Spanish?"

I shook my head and failed to stifle a hoarse cough. She frowned.

"You're ill?"

I said I had been, but was all right now, and she said she could help me with that cough, and that was the beginning of my first large entanglement on the island. We kept on speaking Spanish because my French was rudimentary and she knew little English. Simone was her name, and she managed to mention that her family owned vineyards near Bordeaux. She said she didn't like Americans but I seemed to be a possible exception. We drove downtown in the Citroën, had supper with much wine, and afterward went for coffee and brandy to her large shoreline villa, a prelude to other activity on a carpet in front of a flickering olive-wood fire, none of which seemed to have much to do with my cough except to make it perhaps a bit worse.

(Old John, fifty years later: "Get 'em, boy!")

MARCH 28: Reading Henry Williamson's *Salar the Salmon*. Remarkable observation and knowledge, and the subject matter is intrinsically fascinating to me, but the writing is not so "classic" as reports had led me to believe. A queer mixture of the poetic and the factual, of graceful with rather ungainly prose.

Yesterday spent a while with the Allinghams and Robert Cochrane. It's odd how, without giving a damn about them, I can always get along with this kind of my fellow countrymen—aimless, upper class, usually charming, heavy drinkers. They are really nobodies, although underneath the surface big Cochrane may have a touch of something better. So may Carol Allingham.

Old John: That left only Dick A., of course, and in truth he was and remained a fat-faced, drunken, snobbish, useless representative of the American East Coast Establishment. We got along all right for a while, but then our differences collided.

MARCH 31: Last night to the Jordans', where there was much brandy. A stiffish Yale-type brewery heir and his wife were visiting, and Admiral Pemberton [another American guest, whom I liked] got drunk and unexpectedly blew his top at the heir: "Here's one of the kind of American capitalists I've been wanting to get hold of!" He was in the wrong, but from a decent standpoint, and because I was not involved it was truly comical. The heir went off to bed in a huff and the admiral under criticism from his hosts and his spouse refused to admit any guilt. Dogs and monkeys all over the place.

Headed home, I found a group of fifteen or so Madrid law students in the street, drinking wine from bottles and singing fine provincial songs. I accepted a slug of their wine and some friendly slaps on the back and later, in bed, listened as their singing continued. It kept me awake but I liked it, and ugly Caliban's lovely lines kept running through my head:

> *Be not afear'd. The isle is full of noises,*
> *Sounds, and sweet airs, that give delight and hurt not.*

The visit of the admiral and his wife lasted for a couple of months and we became fairly close. I remembered his name from the Pacific warfare, in which he had been something of a wheel, and I was very fond of Mrs. Pemberton, a thoughtful, well-read, reticent woman from a New England textile family. The admiral was a drinker but usually held it well, and neither of them wanted anything to do with the ambient expatriate colony. In fact, the Jordans themselves began to distance themselves from that crowd while the Pembertons were there.

In April, with the Jordans away, Mrs. Pemberton came down with a strange ailment that caused little pain but sapped her abundant energy and kept her in bed much of the time. One afternoon I ran into the admiral on Plaza Gomila and he said, "I need you at the house this evening. This Spanish doctor is coming over, and I can't ever understand what he says."

I knew the doctor, a decent man named Martorell, and gladly

agreed to serve as interpreter, without reflecting that that task is not always a cheerful one. So at eight o'clock I went over to the Jordans' granite villa, which was always dark inside, even at midday. There I met with the admiral and the doctor in its high-ceilinged living room, with lapdogs underfoot and tiny pet monkeys scampering about on curtains and overhead beams and issuing slow and mournful whoo-whooing cries.

With a fixedly somber face and without preamble, Dr. Martorell told me that his laboratory tests of Mrs. Pemberton's blood and urine samples indicated that she had a rare and untreatable form of circulatory cancer.

I knew he was a very honest man, but I couldn't believe what I was hearing from him. "Are you sure of this?" I said.

"Sí, es cierto," he answered. It is certain.

The admiral's eyes had been flicking back and forth as we spoke, and I told him what the doctor had said.

He had had his evening drinks. After a pause, staring straight into the doctor's face he said belligerently, "What kind of two-bit lab has he got in this Godforsaken place? Tell him what he's saying is a pile of crap!"

Martorell had gotten the message even before I offered my milder translation. He shrugged, nodded to both of us in turn, and left stiff-backed. Above our heads the monkeys kept crying whoo-whoo and defecating small gobbets down onto the carpets and furniture. Pemberton turned his angry face toward me.

"Don't you think I'm right?"

I said, "Admiral, I sure hope you are."

And in fact he was. They flew back to the States soon afterward and had her condition diagnosed, writing to me later. Whatever it turned out to be, it wasn't cancer, and it was very curable. At that time Spanish medicine had a good way to go. . . .

APRIL 10: When you have a woman, it seems always—because she fills so large a gap in you—that you have many friends and acquaintances, more than you can comfortably handle. When the woman is gone, you realize that the acquaintances are desperately few; you want more and you acquire more. Is this perhaps, for a writer at least, an advantage to being womanless? God forbid that I find any more such advantages. . . .

This profound observation had to do with the fact that Simone had gone back to Bordeaux to visit her parents, with her small son from a failed marriage in tow, along with his nursemaid. I was to find that these home visits of hers occurred frequently, and as time went on I came to welcome them somewhat, for she had grown heavily possessive toward me. Once when she had seen me sitting innocently at a sidewalk café table with Marie Colton, she later treated me to a diatribe on faithlessness, which she defined as a specifically American trait. I did not risk further scolding by pointing out that Frenchmen were far worse in such matters.

APRIL 12: Am ambulating vaguely toward the purchase of a sailboat, which may or may not be a good idea but I want one extremely. Talked to Paco Alarcón again last night, about maybe buying his *Melkart* sloop. He gave me information about the evil character of my landlords, corroborating Margarita, who yesterday told me all about servant politics in the Jordan household and let go a good healthy blast at those same landlords of mine, her employers. I still have the ability to make "little" friends like these and that old fisherwoman on the beach yesterday. Knowing the language helps, and my Spanish is back in fair shape by now, about as good as it was in Mexico eight years ago. I can *think* in it again, mistakes and all, and even Margarita's very colloquial chatter has become intelligible.

I had met Paco Alarcón, a slightly built, long-faced, earnest, likable young local, during my rootings around at the Club Náutico in downtown Palma, and will have more to say about him later.

Another person I came to know better during this time was big Robert Cochrane, who turned out to be more interesting than he had seemed while uttering superficial jests at the Jordans' dinner table. He had brought his Plutarch to Spain, for instance, and was obsessed with words and their variant meanings, and with American Southern country music. Huge and muscular and good-natured, he had a gift for rude New York comedy involving things like the brown Spanish toilet tissue of that era, slick on one side and splintery rough on the other. Once at a gathering he kept rubbing his elbow and said he had thrown it out of joint that morning. When someone asked how, Robert said, "I used the wrong side of the paper."

He came from some sort of Irish-contractor moneyed background in New York, had been a bit too young for the war and, oddly, had attended the University of Virginia. I was unable to learn of anything truly useful that he had ever done. Capable of getting along with all sorts of people, especially women, he knew a little about a number of subjects such as bullfights and the music of Hank Williams, and liked the idea of doing things— sailing, starting an English-language newspaper in Palma, motorcycling—without making any moves toward their accomplishment.

When he was serious, as he often was with me, what came through most clearly was lostness, searchingness, a yearning toward meaning and direction. I myself at that time, though not exactly lost, was a searcher too, and I suppose the similarity of our quests helped to draw us together.

APRIL 14: Yesterday a.m. wrote letters home and to Simone in France. In the afternoon the bullfight which wasn't really much—good enough bulls with one horrible butcher (Ybarra?), one rather daring youngster (Posada), and one touted torero (Antoñete), who came through with a little nice muleta work but had one unsatisfactory animal and hashed the other in the killing. It all left a rather bad taste. Funny how easy it is, with only a little experience, to know when that stuff is bad. I am going to keep seeing bullfights until I've witnessed a really good one, then decide whether or not I actually like them.

Have been working regularly though not heavily on the Corporal story. Am going to shorten it radically, do it by scenes and leave gaps between. It stinks of course even as a concept, but maybe it will get me back into the routine of writing. God, I need that (∞).

"The Corporal story," whatever the hell it was and whatever happened to it, turned out to be one of my last attempts at writing slick fiction. . . .

Maybe that ∞ symbol deserves its own note. It is sort of like knocking on wood. I started doodling it in classes at Columbia in the 1940s, somehow decided it must be good luck, and in later years have used it as a cattle brand, a belt buckle, a tie pin, and on my books.

APRIL 16: Am feeling better physically, which makes a difference. Letters from Homer, the Pryor boy, etc. Rereading Gerald Brenan's shorter book, *The Face of Spain,* still good though very Englishly milking every situation of its poetry. He rather frightens me, for I never do that. He is also even fairer minded, more two-sided, than I remembered, despite his basic Republican sympathies. You must be, here.

Am going inexcusably slowly with this story, about one short scene per day, but at least I'm rising early and getting at the typewriter. I amble around in the afternoons talking to Spaniards about boats, etc. There is great confusion about the right price. I'm tempted just to take Paco's boat at 10,000 pesetas, which I can afford [this was about $170 at that time if you exchanged your dollars on the black market, as everyone did], but I don't want to be known around as easily screwed.

Continued revelations of character. Margarita, though most pleasant, is a chatterbox full of gossip. Her talk about her domineering macho gallego brother-in-law. She has a nice little tail and legs and uses them provocatively, but that would be a major mess. The Jordans in their constant bickering, the slow dissolution of a bored and reasonless marriage between two spoiled people. Sarah and her other three husbands she told me about—a sadist, a syphilitic, a homosexual. A commentary not on her luck but on her, and now she has a blue-blooded chorus boy. All these weird little animosities coming to a head. I refuse to involve myself.

Big Cochrane and his Lambie Chuck, Faith Adams, who has showed up from New York, tracking him down. She has tamed him and yet brought out an element of subsurface desperation that didn't show before. He is not so easygoing, and the futile searching is much closer to the surface. Wanting me to move in with them, a very poor idea. A good fellow in his way and I like him, but I'm fairly sure I can't help him.

MAY 4: Some changes. The Jordans have gone away to London in their desperate fashion to have Jim's trick neck attended to, probably not to return. [But they did . . .] The social-obligation luncheon I had on my terrace, with them hacking at each other, and the big land snails (Margarita cooks them beautifully in a sort of creole sauce) pushing the pot lid off as the water heated up, and Cochrane and I and Margarita grabbing them from the kitchen walls and floor and putting them back in the pot, and a dessert of wild strawberries embedded in pyramids of whipped cream.

I am closer to getting the boat and I like the idea better now. Anyhow, I'm heading for a simple life in Andraitx or somewhere, very soon. Cochrane wants to come along, which would be o.k. except that he's not looking for the same thing as I, and simplicity doesn't follow him.

Old John: He was in fact, I had decided, looking for a ride on my shoulders, which was all right except that my shoulders were not broad enough just then. But he was still somehow worth caring about, big Robert.

By May, though, I was caring much less about the expatriate colony in general, for I now knew nearly all of its denizens, and living in their midst it was often impossible to escape their parties, clashes, amours, and perennial gossiping about one another. Fed up, I had begun to think of dashing off a quick, abrasive little novel describing these people and their ways, and made a number of notes in the journal about people and things to include in such a book. These notes are a bit chaotic and often involve persons and events that won't be mentioned again in this memoir but, with apologies, I will set down some paraphrasings of a few of them here to indicate the flavor of my views:

• The period in late April when the sepia—edible cephalopods closely akin to squid—were excitedly breeding, and at night locals in anchored boats were catching them with dip nets, using a light and a string-tethered female to which the males would swarm.

• Paco Alarcón as a monarchist who wouldn't resist communism if it came, because anything would be better than present conditions. And he and Jorge and the other young studs pursuing the tourist chicas from France and Scandinavia, hardly ever achieving their ultimate aim but filled with the joy of the chase.

• Dignified—pompous, really—Commander Berry, USN Retired, who got so drunk at a party that while bowing ceremoniously to a lady he continued forward and downward and banged his head on the floor tiles.

• The considerable group of prosperous, self-centered, middle-aged women drinkers, widowed or divorced, and the Baroness as caterer to their sexual tastes whether standard or lesbian.

• Dr. Martorell as a Spanish observer drawn into the expatriate orbit, finally consenting to operate on Hans the Jordans' dachshund and then being left unpaid.

• Swedish Gerda, a thinking person with much charm and an unhampered view of sexual matters that made her happily available to any man whom she liked, though on the island such men were not numerous.

• The Jordans, over and over, and the Allinghams. Carol A. as someone who was once bright and patrician, now physically ruined and foggy with drink. She has the money, and won't buy Dick the sailboat he wants.

• Cochrane's "Lambie Chuck," Faith Adams, who came here to find him and is still as bewildered by him as she was at home.

• Margarita's servant gossip about the shapely French "sucia" ("the dirty one") and her conquests, one of which involved carnal connection at a party in broad daylight.

• Rich, drink-fuddled Tally Hatcher from Texas with a senile old father in the back of her villa, and the two hangers-on who live with and off of her—evil John Dutchman who I'm sure is a hideout Nazi, and more bearable French John Menard.

• Joe of Joe's Bar, the gentle wise Austrian probably Jewish refugee whose establishment is his refuge here.

• Vicente's nightclub where expatriates mingle amicably with Falangist black-marketeers.

• The cleanness of boats and the sea and the hill villages.

And so on . . . I had the writing compulsion on my back but such a pattern of life was not conducive to work, and the main result of this note-making, later in the summer, was a scathing magazine article, of which more in its place.

In May I moved out of the house next to the Jordans, when the Kuhns, as agreed, came out from Barcelona to take it over. I found a room in downtown Palma to stay in while looking for a flat or a small house. Since the expatriate crowd now didn't know where I was, it was easier to stay loose from them, as well as from Simone, who had come back to the island in May quite a bit more possessive than before. I couldn't make myself stay away from her entirely, for she was very good in bed and I did like her despite her crazy jealousy and, now, her constant complaints about the fact that I wouldn't tell her where I was living.

But I couldn't take a steady dose of her either, especially after she began talking about taking me up to France to meet her parents. Even her Spanish with its throaty r's had begun to grate on my ear.... During this spell I found myself at times skulking about in the city in a sort of tense, low-comic fashion that was not very comical to me. I was especially wary when near the Club Náutico or the Plaza Gomila or other old haunts, checking from around corners for the presence of a Citroën with French plates.

At least she wasn't a part of the American-English-Scandinavian crowd, whom she disliked utterly, so they couldn't get together to flush me out. . . .

After a while I did find a little backstreet terraced house in El Terreno that was being vacated by an Englishwoman, and moved in there without advising any of my fellow aliens or my French lady of its whereabouts. Margarita, the maid from the other house, came and cleaned up for me once a week on her day off from the Kuhns. She was a good friend by now and told me all her troubles, including the fact that whenever she passed near her current boss, Professor Walter Kuhn the eminent authority on Catalan art, she had to scoot by fast to keep him from pinching her tail. Another of her problems was fairly serious. She had gotten herself involved with a black-marketeer-smuggler type who promised to get her to France and took most of what little money she had, ostensibly for that purpose, but did nothing beyond trying to maneuver her into a bedroom. Finally I spoke of this to my friend Pepe Mut (for whom see below), and he pulled some local strings that I didn't want to know about, but at any rate Margarita got her money back and I suspect the lustful and crooked estraperlista may have spent some time in a small dank cell.

Not that all of the estraperlistas were objectionable characters. For changing money, I dealt with a pair of affable brothers to whom Jan Kuhn had sent me, and they were straightforward businessmen, in their dealings at least if not in terms of Spanish legality. After they had decided I was honest too, they would cash my checks on a Texas bank, and I would often linger in their office for a half-hour or so, chatting and answering their questions about America. Ultimately they offered me a free round-trip air ticket home, if I would pick up a certain suitcase there and bring it back to Spain. I knew the thing would be somehow loaded with illicit gold—still held to $35 an ounce in the States, but wildly higher elsewhere—and politely turned down the proposal, a decision they accepted with understanding smiles and nods.

I bought the little 5½-meter Hispania-class keel sloop from Paco Alarcón, who had named it the *Melkart* after a Phoenician god, and got absorbed with fixing it up and learning its quirks. It dated from well before the Spanish Civil War and its boards had a little rot in them here and there, but you couldn't tell that except by probing with a knife blade. After I had spent a week using scrapers and sandpaper and a paintbrush on it, it was smoothly and brilliantly white, with good German varnish on the mahogany brightwork and the spars, a red waterline, and a bottom blue with mercury antifouling paint I had mooched from a friendly American yachtsman in the harbor. And on the usually gentle waters of Palma Bay it proved to be a trustworthy and easy-handling craft. The carefully fitted narrow planks of its hull formed lovely curves, and its cast-iron keel kept it steady in all winds.

Hinterland-born in a time of few big reservoirs, I was by no means a seasoned sailboat man, having come at that pursuit only toward and just after the end of the war, when I discovered a small marina on the post where I was stationed, Camp Lejeune on North Carolina's New River estuary. The marina was stocked with eighteen or twenty small centerboard sloops of three different kinds: Lightnings, Seagulls, and some pretty lapstrake models called Town Class. None of the boats were being used by anyone, and I was invaded by an ambition to learn how to handle them. My commander at that time, a tall, red-headed, good-humored lieutenant colonel from Georgia named Trotti, as

The Melkart

innocent as I of sailboat knowledge, was easily infected with my enthusiasm, and the two bored sergeants in charge of the marina were highly pleased at our interest.

So we started our self-education, sometimes with an instruction book in one hand and a tiller in the other. (I still have a copy of that excellent book, H. A. Calahan's *Learning to Sail,* and must have had it in Palma, for in its margins and other blank spaces are written the Spanish words for boat parts and rigging and nautical terms.)

We had plenty of spare time, especially after the war was over in mid-August, and plenty of mishaps too—breaking spars, going aground, blowing out sails, and once flipping a Town Class over in the middle of the wide river—after each of which events one of the sergeants would chug out in a little outboard and tow us in, with a smile on his face because it was good to see officers foul up, even if he liked us. But by October we were reasonably competent, and that was a satisfying autumn, full of the glad awareness that death and mayhem were behind. The weather was alternately stormy and golden, the smooth tidal river and its shores rich in oysters and crabs and fish and fruit from old plantation orchards. We would take our random harvests to the colonel's quarters for his pleasant wife to prepare. With these meals she would often serve a good salad made of lettuce, cottage cheese, and olives, which Trotti referred to as "pearls," because he said that putting it before his small children, who didn't like it, was like casting pearls before swine. . . .

I had sailed only a little since that period eight years before, but the knowledge came back fast in Mallorca with the *Melkart,* and during this relearning process I made some Spanish friends steeped in the lore of navigating local waters, some of it probably dating back to the Phoenicians or earlier. One little jingle of theirs, very accurate, has stuck with me:

> *Al norte joven o al sur viejo,*
> *No te fíes el pellejo.*

(Don't trust your hide to the young north or the old south winds.)

In the beginning I sailed most often alone, making my mistakes away from the perusal of critical eyes. There were not many such mistakes, and all were minor, for the bay's waters held few hidden dangers and I didn't go out when I distrusted the winds that were blowing. Learning to come back into the Club Náutico's marina without bashing a dock or someone else's boat took a little time, and mattered especially, since in that area plenty of eyes were observing your maneuvers. The winds, after passing over the island's mountains, were usually fitful close to shore, and as you headed along one of the club's entry channels between docks you had to play constantly with the mainsail, letting it swing downwind during the gusts and pulling it in for the slacks, then finally freeing it to spill all its wind while you glided the last few yards, slowing, and turned into your slip with only, you hoped, a gentle bump as the bow touched the dock's fender made of old tires.

When, after two or three previous minor foul-ups, I made this approach just right one day, the vigilant watchers—some of the club's hired marineros and a few youngsters who were always hanging around—started yelling ironically, "Olé! Olé!" We were already friends, though at that point I knew only three or four of their names.

MAY 20, PALMA: Still looking for an apartment, am out of the villa and in a room in a private house downtown where I am agreeably awakened in the mornings by the voices of street peddlers, pregoneros. One cries, "Hey little anjack! Poor old marawhack!" which is my own version of the Mallorquín for I don't know what kinds of fish he has in the baskets on his handcart. Am more or (often) less avoiding Simone. Have been rather luxuriating in solitude, fooling with the boat a little, thinking. I feel rather established now, with no need for drinking and partying, and I believe a big change is at hand. Am going to regularize my life and get to work again. I think I have a better perspective on myself, on people. Have made some messes here but not very bad ones. Am going to get a flat, sail my boat, and *write*.

Have spent a lot of time with Paco lately and still like him, the little man with much dignity and humanity. His mixed feelings about Simone and me and the surly way I acted the last time we were all three together. He likes her and thinks I was rude. I was, I suppose, but it seems I had to be.

My failure here to speculate further about a move to elsewhere on the island indicates that I thought I had more or less escaped the expatriate routine in Palma, and in truth I guess I had escaped, not completely but enough.

Paco Alarcón had become a friend during our negotiations over the boat. There was melancholy in his makeup and he seemed to have only a few friends among other locals. I didn't understand this until much later, when I learned that he came from a family of chuetas or chuetones, people whose ancestors had converted from Judaism to Christianity when Ferdinand and Isabella were expelling all more stubbornly Jewish Sephardim from Spain. There had been widespread suspicion of the chuetas, however, on the grounds that some might have merely pretended to convert. The very name was derived from a word for suet or fat, and was based on a tale that the converts ostentatiously devoured bacon or other pork to demonstrate their sincerity. (With the Inquisition watching, who wouldn't?) At any rate, Spain being immensely resistant to change, some four and a half centuries after those troubles these people were still not fully accepted. There is some hint of this situation in one of George Borrow's nineteenth-century books about the Peninsula.

Later, after I had left Mallorca, Paco wrote to me to say that he was marrying an American girl who had come to the island on a visit. I remember that their plans involved leaving Spain, but I lost track of him soon after that.

MAY 21: [Rosario, the flamenco dancer.] Some of it was too balletish for my (undoubtedly bad) taste, but there was also much great heel-stomping hard-shoe stuff. A button-nosed gypsy face, stocky body. She really has it. One of the better things was built on a García Lorca poem:

> La luna es un pozo chico,
> Las flores no valen nada.
> Lo que valen son tus brazos
> Cuando de noche me abrazan.

Must get hold of his work and read it. Also must put a limit to my stay here; the rest of Spain is too much richer. Will maybe go when the sailing is no longer good here, in the fall.

One morning during that furtive downtown sojourn, having cashed a black-market check the day before, I got up and took the trolley to C'as Catalá to pay Margarita for something she had obtained for me, I forget what. It was very early and there was no risk of meeting Simone or any expatriates. The Kuhns were still asleep when I met Margarita at the door of their house. Afterward I was waiting for an eastbound trolley to carry me back into Palma when I noticed a parked tank truck nearby, of the sort that hauled water to the cisterns of people's villas in the dry season. It had no hood, and I went over to watch the driver as he tinkered with a fuel pump that smelled strongly of gasoline, unlike many of the island's vehicles, including most of its ancient taxicabs, which ran lurchingly on the fumes from a gasógeno, a metal box filled with smoldering almond shells and giving off a pleasant scent. Franco's Spain at that time was woefully short of petroleum products.

Unshaven and fat, the driver glanced at me irritably and got back in the cab to start the motor. As the truck moved off toward town, on a whim I jumped up on the rear bumper and caught a handhold on a ridge of the tank. We cut through cool and hazy morning air past oxcarts full of green produce, laborers walking in groups to their work, shoreline villas, an olive grove with tethered hogs grubbing beneath the silvery trees, a small boy watching over goats on a hillside, the golden Castillo de Bellver, and the Cala Mayor, a principal beach where thrifty French couples, not to waste their vacation expenditures, were already out in bikinis. Then the engine coughed and quit again. The driver got down to tinker with the fuel pump some more, and I went around to watch.

He looked at me, then back at the pump, then back again at me.

I said, "Qué tiene el chisme?" What's wrong with the gadget?

He said, "I saw you in C'as Catalá."

"Possibly."

"How did you get here so fast?"

"I came on a truck," I said, waving toward the rear bumper, and the fat man blinked, then burst into laughter. I ended up riding backward on a front fender and banging my fist on the fuel pump whenever it threatened trouble. We reached downtown without more stops and the driver, still laughing, thanked me and I thanked him and we said goodbye.

The island was sometimes a very good place to be. . . .

MAY 25: Little but hiding from Simone and from erstwhile fellow carousers, sailing, trying to write, a slight cold, going to bed at night. Yesterday I took a really fine boat trip to La Fossa, alone going and with enough scary stuff to make it an adventure. Pleasant farting around there with Spaniards. It did me much good and I have more confidence in the boat and my ability to handle it.

This was when my friendship with Pepe Mut, an islander by birth and blood, a superb boatman, and a captain in the Spanish military, was cemented. He and his younger brother Roberto, both of whom I had known slightly at the Club Náutico and liked, had invited me to go with them and a Spanish friend in their small cabin sloop, the *Pegaso,* to La Fossa, a cove on the uninhabited southeastern shore of Palma Bay where they swam and snorkeled and spearfished. The invitation evidently carried more weight than I had realized (the Muts and their friends had very little to do with foreigners ordinarily, except in terms of pursuing French or Scandinavian tourist girls), and when I did not show up at the designated time, they shoved off without me.

Irritated—I hadn't been all *that* late—I took off after them in my own smaller and much less seaworthy open boat and it was a truly hairy trip, with an abnormally stout onshore headwind that kept pushing me toward the rocks, and seas that half-filled the boat before I got to the cove. I had a scared yet exultant feeling of not giving a God-damn as the jagged yellowish rock bottom (I can still see it) slid by close underneath my keel on the inshore tacks.

When I reached La Fossa the *Pegaso* was anchored near a beach where its three crewmen stood, and I headed toward them. When they started shouting and waving me back, I saw that the cove was rimmed by a shallow reef composed of the jagged rocks, so turning the waterlogged sloop into the wind I tried to study things out.

Pepe Mut swam strongly out to the reef and stood on it, barely up to his knees. "Hay un paso," he called, pointing farther along. There's a passage. "Go out a little and come back and I'll be there to guide you in."

I did, and he was there, and as I passed through the narrow

Resting on the rocks

gap in the grim rocks he grabbed the wire-cable port shroud and swung aboard, sitting on the gunwale with his feet in the cockpit's sloshing water, and grinning at me. "Tienes cojones!" he said. You have balls! "This open barquito in that sea."

I was uncertain of my testicular status at that point, exultation having been replaced by a feeling that I'd been quite a bit more foolish than brave, but after that Pepe and I became good friends without question, to my great benefit. He was a lovely intelligent man with immense humor and a great stock of funny stories, a masculine and honorable person for whom friendship was nearly a religious thing. His acceptance of me also gave me access to a number of other good Spaniards, for he was much respected.

Blue-eyed and strong-jawed, he came from a background that was essentially peasant Mallorquín though somewhat elevated, for his father had been estate manager for one of the local titled families, and he and his brothers and sisters had all been educated well. He swam far out into Palma Bay and back each morning, and smoked two or three packs of Chesterfield cigarettes a day, cheaper there than in the U.S. because they came in illicitly and tax-free from Tangiers—smuggling being a major occupation among the islanders. In fact the king of the smugglers, aged and reclusive Juan March, said by many to be the richest man in Spain, was himself a Mallorquín and still lived there.

Pepe was also a perfectionist about the use of the Spanish language and could not bear my mistakes, correcting them as I made them, no matter how absorbed we were in a discussion. We came from quite different backgrounds and there were areas of philosophy and politics that we didn't attempt to traverse together, but that never seemed to matter. We were friends.

I kept wrangling with myself about the idea of a satirical novel focused on the island's expatriates, and even exchanged letters on the topic with Abe Rothberg, my New York friend from graduate school. He maintained that these people were the stuff of which much worthwhile literature had been made, books like *The Sun Also Rises* and Norman Douglas's *South Wind.* I answered that I couldn't view them thus, couldn't see that the aimless foreigners I had come to know in Palma had the dubious tragic stature of (leaving out central characters) Hemingway's Robert Cohn and Mike Campbell, or Yvonne in *Under the Volcano,* or Douglas's dignified Bishop of Bampopo. Most of the alien inhabitants of El Terreno and C'as Catalá struck me at that point as having come to being nothing on Mallorca from being nothing elsewhere, during all their lives to date.

I admitted, to Abe and to myself, that I had possibly not given Douglas and Hemingway and other writers credit for poetic license, for improving their subjects. But these Mallorcan subjects, in my opinion, would need a godawful lot of improving.

Soon, however, I was rescued from these novelistic perplexities by my agent John Schaffner, to whom I had perhaps also complained about the island. On his own, he got a commission for me from *Holiday* magazine to do an article on the Palma expatriate scene, and I set to work on it with relief.

Reading a map with Pepe Mut aboard the Pegaso

JUNE 10: Reading George Borrow's *The Bible in Spain,* which is a real pleasure and gives me a healthy Anglo-Saxon sense of shame at my own waste of time. What he had done and was doing at my age. The eager, courageous, hardy thrust of the man, the close observation, the linguistic accomplishment. He was quite narrow in some ways, but not in all, and the narrowness may have been a part of his strength.

I'm hoping the inglesa will get out of the house Monday [I was taking it over after her departure], because I'm sick of this room. But I don't know that she is leaving for sure; she's sort of crazy—"Tension," she says. All here seem to be thus.

The nervous Englishwoman did finally leave and I moved into the little house in El Terreno, which had a main room with a couch-bed, a kitchen, a bath, and a small storeroom. Beyond one wall with a high window was a schoolyard from which small girls' voices tinkled during the recess periods. Just after I had moved in, pellets of some sort began to rattle against that window from time to time, distracting me at the typewriter. I thought the lassies had decided to devil me in that fashion, and when it happened I would jump up on a chair to catch them out, but never saw anyone. Finally I determined that the pods on some castor bushes beneath the window were in their season of shedding beans explosively, shooting them in all directions. After that the bombardment, which lasted for only a few days, no longer bothered me and I could enjoy the small voices again.

On the other side of the house lay someone's wide, tree-shaded patio that was seldom used. The place suited me well. I told Simone I had changed quarters again but did not tell her where the new ones were. Sometime later this brought on another emotional outburst, and then a further statement of her determination to get me to France to meet her parents.

I said flatly, "No."

"Why not?"

"Because you want us to get married and I don't."

I might as well have hit her. She gazed at me wide-eyed and started weeping. Which led to an embrace with me patting her shoulder, which led inevitably to her bedroom. . . .

Later, when I was dressing to leave, she spoke from where she lay against the pillows. She said, "I've known what you would say, and I've made you say it. It is my own fault."

So both of us knew that things were over between us. Within a short time she went on another of the trips to her homeland and never came back to the island, at least not during my stay there. I felt bad about having hurt her, but it had been going to happen, sooner or later.

JUNE 13: Finished the expatriate article for *Holiday* magazine. It is disillusioned and ill-tempered but well enough written, though I have no idea if it is the kind of thing they want. When registering it in my record, I was shocked to note how little I have done in nearly a year. It scares me.

JUNE 28: Been working desultorily on the dog-eater story, will finish it this week, but without much satisfaction. Too much Plaza Gomila here, too late hours though little drinking. Life here is a confused mess. Even going to Pamplona seems a tremendous effort, and now there is a letter from Kicker [the nickname of a bright Yale junior, the brother of a woman friend of mine in New York] that may bitch that. I feel as of hemlock I had drunk, etc. The hell with Mallorca.

I did get to Pamplona, an aged upland city of stone buildings, for the Seventh of July fiesta of San Fermín. The city was full of wine-squirting, marching, chanting, fife-playing Navarrese Basques with red scarves around their necks, and hordes of foreigners. With me were two young Yalies, the better of whom (Kicker) lost his virginity gratis to a stout jovial Basque whore in the back room of a tavern and all the Basque drinkers cheered and squirted wine into his mouth from leather botas when he came back out deflowered, though I was elsewhere at the time. I saw Papa Hemingway holding court at a sidewalk table on the main square, and using his sport coat as a cape while still another collegiate American served as bull and charged him. It was the first time he had been back in Spain since the Civil War, and people both Spanish and foreign were going to the table to greet him or introduce themselves. I didn't join them. I had in my mind a vague sort of catalog of established living writers, classified according to whether I would want to know them personally or not, and Hemingway, much as I admired his best work—most bookish Americans of my generation had grown up in his vast shadow—was among the nots.

There was another reason too, a deeper one. I had not yet

proved myself as a writer, a real one, and until I managed that I didn't feel I had a right to impose myself on established authors, however much I might admire their work. At Columbia University in 1948, for instance, I had done my master's thesis on William Faulkner, not a bad effort in comparison with most other examples of that genre. Through some friend, probably Martha Foley, I met Faulkner's editor Saxe Commins, who read some of the thesis and liked it, and asked if I wanted to expand it into a book. I didn't, but he remained friendly and gave me a note of introduction to the great William, since Bryan and I would be passing through Mississippi on our way home to Texas. I intended to use the note—I was always sure I would like Faulkner, even during one of his drinking spells—but ended up not doing it, for the reason given above. And years later while in Palma, knowing that another great writer, Robert Graves, was living only a few miles away in Deyá, I never went near him.

Furthermore, in Pamplona that time, I was experiencing a queer feeling of detachment that might have kept me from speaking to Hemingway even without this inhibition and even if I had thought I would like him. I did not, for instance, have much urge to run with the wild crowd that each morning scampered through the town's streets ahead of the bulls en route to the arena, where in the afternoon the beasts would be killed well or badly by the matadors. Those morning streets in Pamplona were full of not only Basques but American college boys beginning the process of learning that they were not Prince Ernest nor were meant to be, and of Frenchmen Frenchly soaking up sensation, and of God knew who else. I felt little kinship with them. However, I stayed up too late one night with some Basque celebrants and was hauled along at dawn to join the madness. The street was loaded with drunks of all nationalities, and the bulls were a long way behind, and when I stumbled against a clot of Harvard men and fell, I rolled out of the way and stayed there till the bulls had gone by, abruptly sober and a bit ashamed, at nearly thirty-three, to be mixing into other people's childishness. I had enough of my own already.

The festival ended after some good corridas and a couple ruined by thrown pillows and bottles from the inebriated, critical public, and the red-scarfed wine-squirters sang its slow dirge over and over as they began to disperse:

> *Pobre de mí, pobre de mí,*
> *Se acabó la fiesta de San Fermín.*

I bade the Yalies farewell; they were touring the Continent in a VW Beetle which they subsequently demolished on some mountain road. "Steve and I were sick of each other by then," Kicker told me much later. "I was driving and we came up behind a slow car on a curve. I wasn't about to pass it, but Steve said, 'I wouldn't pass that car if I were you.' So I did pass it and a truck was coming."

From there, still in Lord Ernest's shadow, I went alone to fish for trout out of a village named Hecho, high in the Pyrenees above Jaca, an interlude described in a story of mine called "A Valley," which *Sports Illustrated* accepted and paid for but did not publish. (Nor do my sparse records indicate that it appeared elsewhere, until I included it in my collection *A John Graves Reader* in 1996.) That was a wonderful trip. I linked up with an old local pharmacist (part of his stock of medicines consisted of dried newts and toads and things like that), an innocent man who loved fishing and took me up and down the river there, showing me worthwhile stretches where we caught plenty of trout, some very nice ones among them. And I made other friends I would never see again among the residents of the primitive inn where I stayed, who organized a party for me when I left.

Back in Palma, I brooded some more and did a lot of sailing, and at one point had a passenger aboard who somehow did me much good. This was a Spanish courtesan type named Maribel, a nonstop talker and probably a major liar too, but if she was she had a hell of an imagination. I ran into her at the Club Náutico, and we ended up greatly enjoying each other on the *Melkart* for a day and a night or two before she left the island. A journal excerpt:

JULY 27: Somewhere in her thirties, a very fine body, blonde-dyed hair, superb features a bit marked by time. God knows how much of her tale was true, but she told it well, if constantly. Was sixteen when the Civil War started, which if true would make her my own age, and had been married for a year to a pansy marqués. Her mother the daughter of an American diplomat in Madrid, father a captain-general, grandfather a grandee of Spain—"Ocho veces noble!" Quit the marqués and became a model for Balenciaga, causing a scandal in society. With the war, the Reds threw her into jail in Bilbao, and later the Nationalists used her as a spotter and informer, but then threw her in the jug too, why she did not say. She entered Madrid with the Nationalist conquerors as a member of the Auxilio Social (sort of like a franquista USO, I gathered), then later [during World War Two] volunteered to go to Germany with the Legión Azul, though to my knowledge that super-Falangist outfit was decimated by the Russians on the Eastern Front, and she didn't say how she got back to Spain. Has lately been living as the mistress of a rich drunken Swede who likes two or three women in his bed at once, and whom she hates. . . . In the end she did not seem foolish or hysterical at all—there were mutual thanks and regards and a fond goodbye. I really liked the crazy so-and-so.

Pepe Mut had seen us sail away from the Club and later was caustic to me about her, exercising his right as a Spaniard to criticize his own breed. Laughing, I told him she was a marquesa.

"Sí," he said with that wry half-grin of his. "Una marquesa. La Marquesa de Pollatiesa."

The Marchioness of Stiffdick. Nevertheless she was great company, and a healthy contrast to Simone. That was a brief, purgative, jolly, and guiltless romp on the little sloop's scratchy cockpit mat, and beside the anchored boat in the mild moonlit waters of Palma Bay, with nightingales singing from a nearby shore. . . .

And so it went. The boat and the friendships with Spaniards let me separate myself more and more from the stultification of C'as Catalá and El Terreno. On request I revised the expatriate article for *Holiday* and did some other work, and by late summer found myself in a more positive mood.

> AUG. 5: Pepe's troubles. Had supper with him this evening, and after he had told me his worries we had good talk about a little of everything. I like him better and better.

He had somehow managed to fall in love, and the woman was one he had met through me, and with whom I had in fact been mildly involved for a while. This was Marie Colton, a young person of beauty and charm though no overload of intellect. What I had known about her before this talk with Pepe was only the things she had told me about her life up to the present time. In Republican days when she had been a baby, her British father had left her and her French mother on the island, never to return. Marie had grown up there and spoke good Spanish, French, English, and Mallorcan Catalan. Twenty-five years old at this point, she had become a sort of outside member of the expatriate crowd, most of whom liked her because she was personable and well-mannered, and with her languages and knowledge of local matters could often help them with shopping or the resolution of servant problems.

Since I was something of an outsider in those circles myself, or at least dubious about their perennial revelry and uproar, we had gravitated toward each other at parties and sometimes would go sailing in the bay. She had had little formal education and for

Friends aboard the Pegaso

that matter possessed few original ideas, but she had a store of humorous tales about the island scene, and in a clear lilting voice could sing its folk songs, or simple ditties in Andalusian dialect that had been taught to her in childhood by a nurse.

None of the foreign set had met her mother or knew where they lived, though Carol Allingham, a sharp and intuitive woman when not too tipsy, knew something about them which she said was not good, without elucidating. There was in Marie an underlying confused sadness and a kind of questingness that seemed to me to mean she was looking for a man to take her away from whatever it was that saddened her. I liked her but I didn't want to be that man; it could not have been a casual amour, which was about all I thought I was up to at the time. I kept my hands off of her except for one evening when, both of us having taken a bit much wine, there was a sort of adolescent smooching and groping episode, one result of which was that I found out she was not a virgin, though I was far from doing anything about it. After that she began to cling a bit, and I started backing off, often to the extent of hiding from her, as I had from Simone.

The fugitive lover of El Terreno . . .

Pepe had watched us and had even taken us sailing with him on the *Pegaso* a time or two, but I didn't know he was attracted to her until, sensing the change, in quaintly honorable fashion he asked my permission to take her out, which I gladly granted. I would see them on the bay in the *Pegaso* or having supper in some restaurant, and when I would pass their table and speak they would insist that I sit with them. To my relief Marie had begun to treat me just as an old good friend, and her eyes and ears and conversation were directed mainly at Pepe, whose manner toward her was one of amused and somehow respectful affection.

Now, however, that night at supper with me—I remember that we were having broiled baby squid—he needed to unload some worries. He asked bluntly if I had made love to Marie, though without using the stark word "joder" that was so common in male Spaniards' talk.

I answered honestly no, but didn't add that I possibly could have.

He stared down at his clenched hands on the table, and without looking up started telling me the island's gossip about Marie and her mother, which he had clearly known for a long time. It was said that after the English father had left for good, when Marie was very young, the French mother had become the mistress of a member of the local titled nobility, who thereafter supported her and her household. And, the story went on, when Marie had reached sixteen, this man had paid the mother a large sum for the privilege of deflowering her daughter, who had become an additional mistress after that, and might still be.

"I am almost certain it is true," said Pepe with his blue eyes now fixed on my face. "But I don't want to believe it, Zhohn."

I shook my head and looked away, myself convinced that the story was valid, for it explained a lot of things about this girl, and also explained Pepe's torment. Despite his sharp and inquiring mind he was a thoroughly Spanish male with rigid ideas about women, who were inevitably either virtuous or whores, and you did not fall in love with the latter kind.

With his eyes again on his hands he shook his own head. "I have never touched her in that way," he said. "Enamorado I am, yes. And I don't know what to do about it."

Attempting lightness, I said, "Maybe you should have kept on chasing French tourist chicas."

His answering smile was a sad one, but then suddenly he shook his head as if to clear it, grinned at me, and started telling a joke about a village priest and the mayor's wife. . . .

AUG. 6: My birthday—thirty-three long and frequently confused years, but I don't feel too bad about them this year. I'll get somewhere, maybe even close to where I'd like to get. I've done something, though not all I should have done, and life can be beautiful. Right now it ain't but it can be. We'll see, and steady on, old Texas.

I am a fairly average American, it strikes me. How average can you get? Went to public schools and college and fought in part of a war, and my old man is a storekeeper. Thank God for all of that instead of being Long Island and Harvard and snotty. Thank God also for being Southern and Western despite all the Eastern crap we've had shoved down our throats. I can sing the "Freight Train Blues," which are pretty horrible, and "All Around the Water Tank," which ain't, and I can play a few chords on a guitar to go along with them. I can ride a horse and can rope a calf if I have to, though not with all that much skill. I can also understand and respond to decent poetry, shoot birds flying, sail a boat, tie flies and cast them well on the water, write (sometimes), splice rope, speak Spanish and a little French, make friends worth making and some enemies too, drink, fight, fart, and throw rocks.

[Old John: Tut, tut, boy! You weren't still all *that* provincial, were you?]

In the middle of August I left Palma for two or three weeks, going up to Cannes to meet my New York friend Abe Rothberg and his wife Esther, then accompanying them to Milan and Venice, talking all the while. In Venice I saw Hemingway again, in Harry's New York Bar.

From there I went up to Geneva alone for a few days before heading back to Spain on a sort of outlaw bus. The French railroads were strikebound and the French farmers were blocking the highways in sympathy, so we zigzagged southward on back roads and finally reached Cerbère at the border, crossing it to board a Spanish train. It had been a festive if wearing journey. One of the passengers was a non-Spanish-speaking young Swiss mother with a baby, frantic when someone failed to meet our train in Barcelona, so I took her to a hotel and the desk clerk, misinterpreting things, gave us adjoining rooms with an unlocked door between. She was manifestly terrified until I convinced her in halting French that my intentions were not carnal. . . .

This trip was a good break that gave me a little perspective on Palma and the life I had been leading there. Also Abe, bright and caring and probing, had made me do some thinking.

AUG. 14, MILAN: Am enjoying Abe, and having someone for a change to talk to on my own terms, show the Palma expatriate article to. Not entirely on my own terms, of course—he's a

New Yorker, a Jew, and so on—but who the hell can you ever talk to on your own terms, entirely? Sam Hynes is maybe the closest, but he is a Yankee and always has troubles. Never to a woman, even the best.

[Old John: I am grateful that this last incapacity disappeared a bit further along in life. . . .]

Abe has changed for the better through his recent association with big things [he was editing a magazine for the Radio Free Europe people, CIA as it turned out later], proving himself to himself and to others. What a blessed difference from a year and a half ago when he was bitter and self-hating. He is also very human here, a little bit lost linguistically like many of us, but then he has always been human with me.

AUG. 16, VENICE: A friend, a real friend with the beginnings of real wisdom, a largeness of mind and of action that had already started him in big things and would carry him a long way further. And with a minute and penetrating interest in yourself, and (rarer) an ability sometimes to help. . . . His great limitation was a coarseness of utterance that had probably started from being Jewish in an Anglo-Saxon world toward which, for him at any rate, it was necessary to show defiance, Anglo-Saxons being shockable. It was not related to any corresponding foulness of mind, for in actions and attitudes he was basically puritanical, much more so than I. But in his talk it went on and on, and the way things ended was that he became a private sort of friend of mine, one I couldn't share with other, more shockable friends. This in me he mistakenly attributed to his being Jewish, but he accepted it.

These comments on Abe's use of rough language were, of course, as of the 1950s. In later times, I expect he himself is being jolted by the freedom of utterance enjoyed by new generations whether Jewish, Gentile, or California cultistic.

AUG. 17, VENICE: And a couple of blocks away across two bridges was a clean bar where a genuinely great author sat drinking a dry martini at a corner table, an integral member of a set of people who spent much time in the bar and all knew one another's first names. They were wealthy Americans and titled Italians and such, and in his best, leaner days the author had not known many of that kind of people, and perhaps would not have liked the majority of them. Now, however, having bought with accomplishment what they had bought with money or had owned through birth, he seemed to like them very well. They spoke charmingly and could afford to hunt and fish in very special places and do many other interesting things, and they did not embarrass him by considering him to be too important. He found it flattering to be an intimate part of their group. He had ceased being able to write very well, but this did not annul the fact that he had done great work.

In Italy, the feeling of isolation and enforced foreignness because you don't speak the language—a feeling I do not have at all in Spain and only a little in France, where I can always communicate.

AUG. 20, GENEVA: A random thought about Dick Allingham: I did him a favor. I unconfused him. When I first knew him, he told me he had never before known a Texan whom he liked. The fact that he liked me puzzled him and shook his values. Later on I got him to hating me, and this did him a lot of good because he wasn't puzzled any more. Nor had I, for that matter, ever cared greatly for Ivy League Easterners en masse, having believed as an article of faith till I was twelve or thirteen that Yankees were malevolent creatures who had destroyed the world of my forebears. But since then, a bit reconstructed, I had managed to like quite a few of them, some very much, and had lost that simplistic certainty. So maybe it helped me a little bit too, being able to dislike Dick.

The wary friendship I had had with Allingham had collapsed after he tried to appropriate my sailboat, Carol having refused to buy one for him. I had taken him out with me a couple of times in the *Melkart,* then had let him sail it alone one day, for boats were a part of his Connecticut background and he handled them well. But after that he would go out in it whenever he felt like doing so, without seeking permission, so that I often found it gone when I went down to use it. Mild protests did no good, so I finally told the marineros on the dock not to let him have it again. Which led to a fine squabble between us that nearly ended in a fight. . . .

Back from the time abroad, I was somehow more outside of Palma's furors and embroilments. For a time I had a platonic connection—a sort of friendship, I guess it was—with a Swiss nightclub dancer named Brigitte, a tough, handsome, selfish, rather testy lady with problems. Her first love and fiancé had collided with an Alp in his fighter plane, leaving her with a child in her womb which she had had aborted, infuriating the fiancé's family. As a dancer she had been on the nightclub circuit in many countries, including the Middle East. She spoke the usual, for a Swiss, five or six languages, and was thinking now that because she was aging—thirty-two—she might open a dress shop and stop dancing.

There is quite a bit about her in the journal, I don't really know why, except that she fascinated me in an abstract way, for there were not even undertones of sexuality between us. In the end I lent her money to straighten out her affairs and to get back to Switzerland—gave it, rather, for I never heard from her afterward, but it didn't matter.

I was getting to work again, chiefly on the piece about the fishing trip to Hecho in the mountains, after Pamplona. This was at least honest stuff and it felt better than the slick things I had recently been messing with. And another relationship developed, accidentally and improbably, with a "separated" young local woman of good family, there being no divorce in officially Catholic Spain back then.

We met in the Plaza Gomila, where she was at an outdoor table, under the plane trees, with a local couple whom I knew from the Club Náutico. They invited me to sit down and introduced me to their companion, a trim, aquiline, dark-eyed lady in her mid- to late twenties. There was conversation of a usual inconsequential sort between me and the couple, chiefly about boats and their owners, but there was also a current between me and the dark-eyed one, who spoke little. I used to think of this as electricity. . . . After a time the couple saw some friends across the plaza and excused themselves to go say hello, and the lady looked me full in the face for the first time.

"Why are you here, on this island?" she asked in a somewhat accusatory tone, using the formal word "usted" though I was "tú" to her friends.

I said I was a writer and it didn't matter much where I was, and I liked the island, at least for now.

"Where are you living?"

I told her, as I had told few persons.

Suddenly she smiled. "Conozco aquella casita," she said. I know that little house. "It's on the next street over from my mother's home, where I live."

"We'll have to visit, then."

Shaking her head and looking down, but still with a small smile, she said, "No conviene." It wasn't suitable.

The couple returned to the table and that was the end of that, but a few days later I met her on the sidewalk of my own street and we exchanged greetings though little else, for she was clearly uneasy about being seen alone with me in public. Then one evening after dusk, astoundingly, she came to my house and knocked, having seen a light through the glassed door and me alone within, at the typewriter.

I let her in. She was embarrassed but game, and pulled the

door's curtains shut. "I think . . . I think you are someone I can talk to," she said, using the "tú." "I think we can communicate."

We could, and did so at length. Her name was Magdalena, rendered Lena, and she had a wealth of sorrows and frustrations to unload and, with a listener not linked to the island's social web, poured out a few of them that evening. Then she wanted to know about my own life and messes and motivations.

We talked until she looked at her watch, shook her head, and stood up. "Ya basta!" she said. "Thank you for listening to me."

And left, after carefully peering out at the dark street for people who might see her emerge.

Her story, which she amplified on subsequent visits, was a usual one but only up to a point. When quite young, she had had a novio, or fiancé, and as frequently then, with the miserable economics of post–Civil War Spain and consequent protracted engagements, she and the novio had been fully intimate. But when she had learned he was cheating with someone else, she had angrily broken with him, and thereafter as a practically certifiable non-virgin she was no longer negotiable in the Palma marriage market. Thus, a strong character, she went to southern France where her family had business connections, found an apparently suitable Frenchman, and married him. But he turned out to be a disaster, sexually and financially and temperamentally, and after the marriage collapsed she came back home to exist in the limbo of the separada.

These further visits from her did not involve mere talk, for the current was still running between us. She had not been with another man since the Frenchman. Everything we did had to be circumspect and nocturnal, because in her world such women were required to keep up appearances more than anyone else, and by then I was sharply aware of how fast and viciously gossip traveled in that place. We both knew too that our relationship was just for the brief remaining time I would have on the island, and there was no question of long-term attachment or marriage.

Not only did she have the local strictures riding on her back, but in her own very Catholic mind she was married for life to that sorry Frenchman whom she would never see again.

But it was powerful for all that, and not in the least neurotic. She had a slim responsive body and a wry earthy intelligence, and what we had together was badly needed by us both, not just in physical terms. None of the other "love" I had found on the island, even that with Simone, had been much more than animal release.

In October I went to Madrid briefly on a sort of reconnaissance for the November move.

AUG. 29, PALMA: Sitting in the Bar Bellver at 10:30 a.m., waiting for your café con leche and croissants, checking the comically moral front page of the newspaper *Baleares*—"In Spain Harmony between Church and State Is a Reality"—and a girl walks in through the grass-chenille strings of the fly door. You notice her as you do notice girls—dark, perhaps French but probably too handsome for that, with a blue blouse and slacks and her hair cut short in the French cut that, when it looks good at all, looks good on Spanish women with their thick dark hair. She goes to the door of the lavatory and tries it. It is locked, and she puts her left forearm against the wall and leans her brow on it and begins to sob, beating at the wall with her free hand. You think that she must know the proprietress and the others and that it is a joke, pretending great distress at not being able to pee promptly. But it isn't. Other women go to her with soothing sounds, and you ask the waiter who comes finally if you should go outside.

He says no. "There was a motorcycle accident."

"Someone was hurt?"

"Hurt, no. Dead."

It turns out that the impresario of the Tito's nightclub band has flipped his big, powerful, inferiority-complex Harley-

Davidson at 4:00 a.m. and has killed himself, and this is his girlfriend. Everybody including you is much depressed and the waiter forgets to add hot milk to your coffee and goes off to talk about the accident, while the girl sobs wildly at a corner table, comforted by women she does not know.

SEPT. 4: Said goodbye today to Marie. She is going to the States with this pleasant Minton couple from Virginia, who have been charmed by her. I don't really think she'll get straightened out, not at 25, but she will possibly find a good chump American for a husband who will believe, with luck forever, that he has acquired a romantic prize.

She did not find such an American, but ended up back in Palma after I had left the island, and I didn't see her again. The next winter when I was living in Madrid and Pepe Mut was there also, he never mentioned Marie, and I sensed that he had broken with her at some point after that supper conversation of ours, for I doubted she would have gone off to America while he was still potentially the supportive man she was looking for. Nor would she have written me a couple of rather tender letters from the States, as she later had.

Two or three years afterward, back at home in Texas, I got a letter from Pepe with news about the island and things he had been doing, and one short, bitter paragraph concerning Marie. He had lately seen her, he wrote, in the Plaza Gomila in a group of "las de cuatrocientas"—four-hundred-peseta whores, a fairly hefty price at the time. . . .

SEPT. 6: Perhaps if you lack a flowing and towerbuilding imagination—and I think I've demonstrated this lack in the lousy slick stories I have been writing lately—perhaps in such a case what you do is to live hard and much and then put down what happened with just a few sharpening changes. I think

Hemingway has been mainly thus. The trouble with me is that I tarry too long in the living and never get around to the writing. . . .

Quite possibly if the Republicans had won, Spain would soon have become, as conservatives take for granted, a Soviet substate, and then it would certainly have been worse, far worse, than now. This consideration does not, however, make more palatable the blue-shirted Falangist gentry who lord it in the barrera seats at the bullring and at Vicente's nightclub, or the utter absence of the old civilized Latin humanists, or the entire hatred in the eyes of Andalusian peasants directed at anyone in a coat and tie.

SEPT. 10: Am working on the Hecho fishing story and think it will turn out. News from Schaffner that *Holiday* is still very pleased with the expatriate piece and wants more, also that he has placed "The Laughter from the Western Islands" [another of my "real" short stories] with a little magazine—at minimal if any pay, of course.

SEPT. 15: Lena came back to Palma after the French breakup to live with her widowed mother and help administer the family's property, in the sort of half-world of more-than-complete virtue expected of the separada. . . . I seem at least to be learning a few things about people lately, especially women.

SEPT. 20: Odd crossed wires of the sort that turn up here. Lena's former novio is the tall, likable, masculine type whom Brigitte insulted when he laughed at her damned little poodle You-You, and who also (Lena says) is putting the horns on amiable, drunken Francis Pantino the erstwhile California lawyer. I get again the sense of the intense scrutiny we aliens receive from the locals, who outwardly seem to be paying us no attention at all. Cf. Margarita and all that servant gossip she has relayed to me. Lena, who has no other direct contact with the foreigners than me, but who undoubtedly gets gossip from her own friends and servants, is also aware of my former links with Brigitte and Marie Colton, and clearly, very Spanishly, has a hard time believing me when I tell her there has been nothing between myself and them. And of course the locals scrutinize one another all to hell, as Lena does that ex-novio and as they have all done forever with Marie and her mother and their aristocratic provider.

SEPT. 23: Am working better, and within a few days will have finished a draft of the Hecho piece, which I think will revise well, good enough to be sent out. What then? Worry about that when it comes. When I get away from here to Madrid soon, things ought to start clarifying themselves.

One afternoon at Joe's Bar I got to talking casually with Lena's former novio, a big easygoing man named Rafael Montjuich with whom I had had slight but cordial acquaintance for a good while. He had no idea, of course, that I knew her. Seated beside us at the bar was a little rat-faced local with a Falangist pin in his buttonhole, half-drunk, who knew Rafael and kept butting into our conversation while we tried to ignore him.

Finally this character poked his finger into my shoulder and said, "Tú! Yanqui! When your countrymen come to the island with their wives, why do they let the wives go to bed with Spaniards?"

I said I didn't know about that, but if true it likely meant only that there were fools of all breeds, and I pointed at him—"Hay tontos de todas las cepas."

Pure hatred flowed from his eyes to mine, but Rafael clapped me on the shoulder and laughed a big laugh, repeating my phrase over and over, delighted that I had put the bastard down.

I was sort of proud of myself too, for being able to do it in Spanish. . . .

Lena that night, half-humorously, mused over the possibility of pregnancy and said that if she did get that way she thought she would go to France and have the child, then bring it back here to raise.

"Do you want a child?" I asked her.

She turned serious. "Sí, mucho," she said.

"But I won't be here much longer."

"Así? And what could you do if you were? I would give the niño the surname of my adorable French spouse."

SEPT. 25: Yesterday and the night before with Cochrane and his Faith, visiting and drinking a little too much. He was on one of his lows and kept talking about it. The depth of his lostness—he has never done *anything* that mattered. He says now that he's thinking he might go join up with the French in Indo-China or try for a job in the Arabian oil fields, meaning it.

I am discouraged by the apparent impossibility of his pulling out of this expatriate pattern. Like me he came far from home with the idea of getting his head on straight, and probably it is the similarity of our quests that has made us friends. But it isn't working for him, because he has no specific aim to carry it along. Is it working for me? More, yes.

Faith wanted me to take him over. "You could straighten him out," she said when we were briefly alone. "I know you could. He listens to you."

I shook my head. "Nice lady," I said, "I've got all I can handle just trying to get myself straightened out."

But I did like the big guy.

SEPT. 28: Today it has been raining steadily, and while I was having a sandwich in Joe's Bar, French John Menard came in with the news that Tally Hatcher, the rich drinking Texas lady, has been murdered by her other resident hanger-on, Dutch John.

When French John made this announcement, pale and nervous and asking for brandy, nobody was in the bar but Joe and me and a Nordic couple quietly talking in their own language at a corner table.

Menard was a drinker only of wine in my recollection, but he tossed off the brandy and shoved the glass toward Joe, who refilled it. Both of us were watching him with questions on our faces.

I didn't know French John's personal history, nor did anyone else seem to, but his accented English was fair, with an American flavor. "The bastard he's drunk, like always," he said. "She too, a little, and she scold him about something and he grab a big ashtray—you remember that ashtray?"

I nodded, having glimpsed it on one of my rare visits to her house; it was solid cast brass with gargoyles around its rim, and must have weighed six or eight pounds.

"Well, he bop it hard on her head. She fall, and I get down and feel for the pulse and look at the eyes, and she's dead, all right. Then I look at that damn Nazi and when I see his face I get up and run out and go to the police station."

"He *is* German, then," I said.

"Oh, yeah. The worst kind."

Mrs. Hatcher and I, both Texans, had never been at all close, in part because I couldn't stand Dutch John, and also because I was and still am uneasy around true alcoholics, although (or maybe because) there have been a few among my friends and relatives. She was a faded blonde in her forties with West Texas oil money in the background. She spoke in a way that indicated an expensive education, was kind to her senile father, and had created a thoroughly evil situation for herself on the island with, finally, this sad and ugly conclusion.

And all of that was a sort of dirty, logical, end-of-the-season happening to hear about in a dimly lit bar on a rainy day in a foreign land. Pepe Mut, who knew the local police officials, told me much later that Dutch John had eluded capture for a time, going to the mainland and scooting about from place to place, but had finally been taken, given a trial at which French John was the chief and probably only witness, and condemned to life in prison.

I never heard what happened to the old father, who by report had always sat placidly smiling in the rear of the house, with a servant to attend him.

SEPT. 30: The rain continues, sad yet in a good way. Without the pull of the hot blue outside and the boat and the lovely water, it is possible to think clearly. I slept an hour this afternoon and woke contentedly and sadly to work and more or less finish the Hecho piece, which needs much trimming and rearranging but I think will do most of what I wanted it to do.

I will go to Madrid and will write a book and it will be good. Sadly, clearly, I know this today, the big bird of Destiny still on my shoulder, sad too but digging in his claws. It's coming late and it won't be as good as it should be, as it would have been earlier, but it's there. Yes.

[Old John: All this sad optimism turned out to be quite premature. You hadn't made it yet, kid.]

OCT. 2: Working still, not sailing. Next week to Madrid to scout it out for the move. The Hecho story is finished and not bad, though who will buy it? Maybe *The New Yorker,* or *Holiday* (∞).

When Lena came around the evening before I left for Madrid, she said it would be the last time.

"Why?" I asked. "I'll be back in a week or so."

"Only until you leave again. It is better to end it now."

She spoke sadly and affectionately, and I couldn't answer. She knew she was being pushed back into limbo, too young. There was little likelihood of another chance and safe and warm liaison like the one with me, and maybe having known that warmth and safety would make limbo worse this time.

"I don't know," she said. "I've had bad luck with men, just bad luck. Two horrorosos."

She didn't mean me, but her novio Rafael and then the French husband.

"There's still some time left."

She shook her head, then stared solemnly at me. "Tell me. What will I do, when you've left?"

And I didn't know.

OCT. 10, MADRID: The first night here on this exploratory jaunt, having embarked tentatively, as one who wets his foot, upon another of my periodic and deliberate uprootings. Alone, really alone and not knowing anybody in a big foreign city, a little diarrheic, a little daunted. Because now I've got to work things out here, and though they will work out, there is a lot of lonesomeness at first. Because that's the way you do things.

OCT. 11: Another rainy, mildly belly-ached day. Poked around a little in the Prado re-examining Bosch and Goya, and then by mistake, thinking it was a show of Spanish dances, went to a stage drama called *El Baile,* with Conchita Montes. A senti-mental comedy affirming the basic middle-class values, with a number of laughs. Was pleased at how well I understood prac-tically all of it. And God bless the middle classes anyhow, for being sentimental and yearning for decency and for innocence, which do sometimes exist. Their virtues are those, and their shortcomings too. . . .

Bosch—God, how he hated and loved life, and people. As close to Swift as a painter can get. And looking at Goya's

Dibujos—people like Steig and this Abner Dean are weak imitators. And the godawfully Spanish faces in Velásquez's *Los Borrachos.*

OCT. 13: A stage show last night: Luisa Ortega with Manolo Caracol, her father, who plays the guitar and wails out the cante jondo while she dances. At first I thought she had gotten worse, or that my last spring's impression was faulty. Then they started the pure flamenco and it was what it was supposed to be. The wizened Spaniard seated on my left didn't think so, however, and kept bitching all the way through for some obscure personal reason, indignant at the applause, shaking his fist and yelling, "Ya está bien, hombre! Ya está bien!" With me was a young Midwesterner named O'Meara, pleasant though not overburdened with brains, with whom I had taken up at the hotel as I tend to do after a day or so of silent lone travel. Gave him an earful of Spain, which he liked o.k.

Inside most of today, and the belly pains are keeping me from drinking much besides red wine. At least have gotten off a lot of letters and postcards, bringing my correspondence up to date. This hotel is a pure tourist trap, but I am too lazy and dispirited to change to another. The weather is not even good enough for an excursion to Toledo. No writing, naturally.

OCT. 14: Was talking with an agreeable inglés in the shipping business last night in the bar downstairs, when little O'Meara entered drunk with two really grossly drunk and profanely raucous American merchant seamen and an embarrassed Spanish whore. O'Meara came over and was almost crying with rage about the slob sailors he had gotten himself tangled up with.

"I wish I had old Nicolai with me," he said. "He'd knock their God-damn heads together!"

The Englishman was a little amused and a little uncomfortable and went off to bed. He had told me that Gracie Fields was the one who made Capri into a tourist mecca. Didn't Norman Douglas have as much to do with it? And Axel Munthe? Maybe not, for my Brit was talking about regular tourists, not literary ones who seldom throng.

This evening a very poor musical and dance show, with a Hollywoodish type named Estrellita Castro bastardizing the genre. One fairly rousing loud mass jota, and the rest was a bore.

The results of that first Madrid trip were few—I bought some cloth to have made into suits and sportcoats, wandered around, drank a little wine and brandy with various Englishmen in the city on business, exchanged pleasantries with a few jolly whores of the upper-grade Bar Chicote category, saw some stage shows, was stunned by the superb Prado collections. . . . I looked up none of the people whose names had been given me—that could come later—although I did go to the U.S. Embassy to ask about a cousin's West Pointer husband, one of the Doolittle pilots, who was—or, it turned out, had been—military air attaché. Then I took a plane back to Palma, more or less satisfied. I had some of the feel of the capital and it was a good feel, and when I came back in November I would arrive as less of a bewildered stranger.

OCT. 20, PALMA: Having clothes made, other details, biding my time. . . . Sam Hynes is to be in England this winter. Marie is still writing sentimental notes from Lynchburg—I guess that will stop when she gets my letter from Madrid. Haven't seen Pepe. Rain. Boredom.

OCT. 21: After one of the least pleasant evenings I can remember, watching big Cochrane go ape in Joe's Bar and batter the hell out of three people, a couple of them not bad types at all. I tried to stop him but it was like trying to stop a tank, though I

did keep the second bout, with a likable young American soldier named McHugh, from being more than a one-lick
affair. . . . I feel guilty about the whole thing, though my only
role in the actual brawl was that of an unavailing pacificator.
But I am certain Cochrane's explosion stemmed from my having shown him earlier, when he was sober, the carbon copy of
my expatriate piece for *Holiday,* which turned him guilty and
combative. . . .

When he had finished reading the typescript he slapped it
down on a table and glared at me. "I didn't know you could
write that well," he said.

"Sometimes I can," I said.

"I didn't know you were that God-damned mean, either."

"Also only sometimes."

"Charity!" he almost shouted. "You need a lot more charity!"

But he soon calmed down, or seemed to, and we went out to
Joe's where he got rapidly drunk and proved himself to be
meaner, physically at least, than I had ever thought of being.

The next day I thumbed through the typescript to a passage
where I had seen him pause in his reading, and saw why he had
done so. It was not nearly as caustic as much of the rest of the
essay, but it was about himself. This is it:

. . . As drinking usually does, this leads to a certain monotony, a negativeness in their conversations, their thinking,
and their activities. On the other hand, however, it makes
monotony not only bearable but desirable. One man, an
interesting type with a dormant but genuine intelligence,
who somehow had drifted to Palma and stuck, told me
that he had given up reading anything but magazines; he
found it impossible now to finish a book. The worst of it
was, he said, not looking worried as he spoke the words,
that he didn't care a damn.

OCT. 23: After eight months on this island I handle a sailboat better, speak smoother Spanish, and have added to my life-lists of women and of friends, though Lena is the only one of the former who matters to me at all, and Pepe is the main one of the latter (*damn* Cochrane's complexities!). Only a little work done.

Sailing alone yesterday with a melancholy-exultant autumnal feel in the air, a steady mild westerly wind, a teeming run of mackerel in the bay and trolling for them with a spoon and a thick handline and actually catching three small ones for supper. . . .

Reading: Cela, *Pabellón de Reposo.* Overdone and falsely dramatic, but the reading is good for my Spanish. Joyce Cary, *Mister Johnson.* Sketchily read but enjoyed in the rather detached way I enjoy Cary. All of his people seem emotional to the point of exaggeration.

Faulkner, for all the miraculous knowledge and feeling he gained by staying close to home, perhaps lost some things by it too. Like seeing everything Southern as ridden with the guilt of Negro suppression. Nonsense. What age or place was ever free of that sort of guilt if you wanted to feel guilty?

Old John doubts this glib observation now, in a time when such felt guilt on the part of white Americans—Northern and Southern and Eastern and Western—has wrought large and inevitable changes. . . .

That was the end of Mallorca for me, really, though I would go back there once in the following year for a cruise to Ibiza with Pepe Mut on his *Pegaso.* I sold my own boat back to Paco Alarcón for the same amount I had paid him, though I could by then have sold it for a good deal more to another foreigner. Thus six months' use of that decaying but graceful little craft, a major and lovely dimension in my life on the island, ended up costing me only the price of a new set of sails and some ropes and a few other furbishments.

.The expatriate colony had changed quite a bit during my stay, losing some members who drifted off homeward or elsewhere, and taking on new recruits of much the same types. The ones I still knew I said goodbye to on friendly terms, feeling a little guilt about the *Holiday* article that would hit them in the faces that winter. My relations with big Cochrane had been a bit strained since the violent night in Joe's Bar, but we were still friends and he said he would come to see me in Madrid, which was not necessarily a prospect to be viewed with joy. Pepe Mut was going there too a little later—it was the period when Eisenhower's government was courting General Franco in order to be granted Cold War air and naval bases in Spain and, for liaison, officers like Pepe who knew a little English were being sent to take courses in the capital to improve their command of that language and their ability to teach it to their troops.

He and I would often resolve to spend a day speaking only English, to give him practice, but then we would get interested in what we were saying and would drop back into Castilian. . . .

Dark-eyed Lena stuck to what she had told me and did not come again before I left this second time, nor under the tacit

San Antonio Harbor, Ibiza

terms of our connection, did I have any way to communicate with her. But I understood it, for she had much pride and would not cling when she knew that things were ending. I cared deeply for her and I think she felt the same way toward me, though neither of us had ever expressed this sentiment fully in words. I have always hoped that she escaped somehow from the high-walled box she was in, but I never knew. I couldn't even talk about her with Pepe, as close as he and I were then and later, because he was a part of the Spanish social and religious framework in which she was trapped, and he would not have been tolerant of her situation and her relationship with me.

In fact, I never talked about her with anybody at all.

FIVE

Mainly Madrid

(1953–1954)

I N THE CAPITAL CITY I started out in another nondescript
hotel, as seems to have been my custom, and—a custom too,
more or less—fell in with the first decent person with any
brains whom I encountered there, a young San Francisco Navy
veteran named Kirchen, divorced and adrift. His conversation
and outlook had a boppish California flavor—witchcraft and
Dianetics, marijuana, chicks, cats, spades, and ofays. But he had
come to realize that that world was not enough, and was in
Europe, like myself and most other wandering Americans I was
drawn to, in search of a new self. We cruised some bars together
and took in a couple of stage shows and once, having located a
source of hashish in Madrid, he asked if I wanted to try some. I
told him that alcohol and tobacco were pleasure and poison
enough for me. After a few days he moved on to Italy to continue
his quest.

New self or not, his ultimate ambition, he had revealed when
drinking, was to own a house in Sausalito. . . .

During those early days in Madrid I developed a remarkably
sudden sense of guilt about the forthcoming *Holiday* expatriate
article. I felt as though I had left Palma under a cloud, and con-
templated writing the Jordans, at least, to "let them in" on things
and ease the jolt. But I don't remember that I followed through
on this impulse.

Settling in, I started looking up some of the people whose names had been given me.

NOV. 12: Yesterday I had a drink with Ivan Smirnov [a dynamic White Russian who had been instrumental in founding KLM Royal Dutch Airlines, though I don't remember what connection had put me in touch with him], a mature man of action and much experience and sophistication, a little past his prime, somehow hard for me to talk to. Then, almost unwillingly, I called on Jan Kuhn's recommended Pepe Weissberger, who turned out to be a delicate, aged, bronchitic, gentle, wise Jew of the finest Old World type. Knows literature inside and out, loaded me with books, and will be a superb person to know. It is something to meet again with an actual mature, utilized intelligence. I must say that five days here have been infinitely more full of such experience than any five days I knew on Mallorca.

I did later see more of Señor Weissberger and we became friends, but I seem not to have recorded anything about those later visits, which I recall as warm and stimulating and always rich with book talk. This is one of the journal's large gaps.

NOV. 17: A grandfather [mine, in South Texas] who partook of the virtues and shortcomings of his age, a strong figure and not folksy, who would stand face to face with anyone in the world, knowing himself an equal.

From a Spanish newspaper: "Todo hombre fuera de su país es un poco niño." Outside of his own country every man is something of a child. An excruciatingly accurate observation from an unexpected source. Another shade would be that outside of your own context you are half-assed. If you have no context at all, you're no-assed.

DEC. 6: Two particular faces I've seen in Spain that stick with me: that of an old man selling cheap china Virgins in a street in Granada on a windy, rainy night, and the leathery one of a man in a suit that did not fit him, unashamed to weep while watching Antonio dance. Some weep at bullfights too, when they're very good. Weeping over beauty is something I comprehend, my own weakness in this respect being mainly for lovely and potent language. Increasingly as I grow older, I find it hard to read strong poetry or superlative prose aloud without a prickle in my tear ducts or even a sob.

I was not talking about "message" but about the music of words. The same feeling affects me now when I listen to certain passages of Mozart (who came down, a friend of mine asserts, from God). It even hits me with some popular music, for instance good bluegrass and the songs of Patsy Cline, though that may be just a matter of the increasing sentimentality of age. . . .

DEC. 8: Saw Antonio's onetime partner Rosario dance tonight and was much disappointed. She is aging and the show is "cute" rather than tragic or exultant. This is saddening, because not long ago I saw her and thought she was great. Maybe she was, that time.

Time is moving along and I am farting around, writing halfassedly on insignificant stuff.

This last bit is only one of dozens of complaints about my work habits that characterize the journal. I was by then living at the Hotel Luxor, a small first-class establishment occupying the top three floors of a six-story office building on a wide principal street still called the Gran Vía by everyone, despite its official renaming as the Avenida José Antonio, after the slain founder of the Falange Español. The Luxor was a good place, well run, and I stayed there most of the time for a year, getting to know all the chambermaids and waiters and desk clerks and barmen and becoming friendly with the owner, Gustavo Morales, a nonpracticing dentist originally from the province of Asturias on the Cantabrian coast, where he once took me.

The little hotel had an interesting mixed clientele. There were a good many European and Latin American show people who had dancing and singing and novelty acts aimed mainly at nightclubs. There was a little group of good unaristocratic Englishmen, engineers, who were supervising the repair of old De Havilland engines for Franco's air force. Some solid Spanish burgesses, not big shots, came there from various provincial capitals to do business in Madrid, and now and then American construction contractors and heavy-machinery men showed up, in anticipation of the new American air bases.

The small bar and grill at the front of the hotel served fine breakfasts and could always provide a fillet with salad and potatoes at other hours. Its windows opened on the Gran Vía, and through them on occasion you could get a bird's-eye view of Franco's fancy Moorish Guard escorting the coach of some new diplomat on his way to the Palace to present his papers. The Moors were robed in specific vivid colors for each individual troop, and all their prancing horses had been similarly sorted into blacks, bays, dapple-grays, and duns. Behind the procession always walked two little men with brooms and big dustpans, sweeping up the rich dung.

The window of my own rear room on the fourth floor of the building opened above a small backstreet that was usually quiet, though it had a cantina that would occasionally spew forth a late-night group of quarreling or singing drunks. One time well after midnight the noise got to sounding serious, with women yelling, and I went from my bed to look. A clot of fifteen or eighteen people stood in the middle of the narrow street, dim in the glow of the cantina from which they had come. In the clot's center two women were shouting vile names and slapping each other and pulling hair.

In a Madrid café

Suddenly I saw the glint of a knife and the clot swelled into a circle as people backed frantically away, the two women still in the center but one now lying twistedly flat and motionless and the other, holding the knife, standing over her. Then everybody left, hurrying off in both directions, and there was only the woman's body on the cobblestones, seeming very dead from where I was, four stories up. A couple of men in aprons came out of the cantina and looked at the body with exclamations, and later from my bed I heard official-sounding voices below, but none of it seemed to have much to do with me. . . .

Two other types who showed up at the Luxor were young French encyclopedia salesmen, an ill-matched but attractive pair. We communicated in Spanish because their English was even worse than my French, and if their throaty r's brought Simone very often to mind, I managed to stand it. One was

Jacques Falaise, son of a Socialist deputy, and the other was Jean-Marie d'Oloron, a vicomte out of a family of impoverished nobility—though their title, as Socialist Jacques once pointed out to me in private with snobbish asperity, was only Napoleonic. My friendship with these two began when I steered them toward some reasonable Spanish wine, and flowered when I told them that Spanish Pernod, unlike the denatured French equivalent, was still the true and blissful absinthe, full of logwood and bad dreams. I didn't like the stuff or its effects, but Jean-Marie in particular would stare in fascination as the absinthe turned cloudy in one of those special dripping-glasses, and would toss off glass after glass, ending up insanely zonked and going off usually with some ratty whore over protests from me and Jacques.

They had a chugging little Renault Deux-Chevaux with a floppy canvas top, and since I was going to London that year to spend Christmas with Sam Hynes and his family (he was over there from Swarthmore for a year on a Fulbright scholarship), I rode as far as Paris with them and it was a great trip. They taught me the tunes and words to a number of bawdy French drinking songs that I wish I still remembered, and we ate beautifully and cheaply in the towns we passed through along the way. One special place was Dax, an ancient spa not far north of the French-Spanish border, where we arrived on a cold night and the boiling-hot spring water running in all the gutters and sewers had enveloped the town in swirling fog, a spectral scene. In Paris we partied and dined together a bit and I met Jacques's buxom girlfriend Marthe and Jean-Marie's austere, Napoleonically blue-blooded parents the count and countess, who dwelt in a shabby old house with threadbare carpets and furniture but dressed with antique formality and called each other by the formal pronoun "vous" in front of other people. Then J. and J.-M. disappeared into their own holiday orbits and I waited for a plane to London.

DEC. 19, PARIS: Am in a better frame of mind. Before leaving Madrid I finished the "Alley" story after one and a half years, not too badly I think, and did a first draft of the comic French piece. Am on my way to Christmas in England with Sam Hynes and Liz. France is much more pleasant if you're traveling with Frenchmen. Paris is nicer too but I am of course now alone.

Cochrane in Madrid. He came there seeking guidance, wanting more or less to put himself in my hands, and I told him he ought to go back to New York where at least in some ways he fitted in.

"No, I don't," he said.

"Better than here, anyhow."

"Yes, maybe a little better than here," he agreed.

More and more this "every man out of his country is something of a child" thing is impressing me. Nearly all of us Americans are half-assed over here, possibly excepting those who are rich enough to buy their way along the upper surface of things. Yet it is oddly necessary to get outside your own country in order to see it whole. Me and the Texan at the Luxor, both of us out of the same frame of reference but in different ways, and clashing like that.

That particular short squabble had been just a verbal one. The Texan was a construction engineer or something like that, a tad drunk, with vehement objections to arty types who hung out in foreign places, which he was enlarging upon to a companion in the lobby while glancing occasionally at me, seated nearby with a newspaper. "Writers? Painters? Bunch of God-damn fairies if you ask me," he declared at one point.

Besides his accent I had recognized his Texas A&M ring, so I borrowed lines from an old joke when I answered the not very indirect attack, leaning forward over my paper and looking at him: "You're an Aggie, aren't you?"

He glared. "How the hell did you know that?"

"I saw your class ring while you were picking your nose," I said, which got him more stirred up still, but the large fellow he was with pushed him down in his chair and kept matters from metamorphosing into fisticuffs.

There are no journal entries made during the visit to London, just two or three retrospective notes like the one below.

JAN. 4, 1954, PARIS: London was a lot of things. Sam as fine as ever, still suffering, not allowing himself any freedom if he can't have it all. He and I wandered much through the city, talking, disagreeing, agreeing. Cold and fog and steak-and-mushroom pies in pubs and seeing *All's Well* and *Lear* at the Old Vic. With his genuine scholarly focus on English literature, he is much more in our own cultural line of things than I am in Spain, yet Spain does suit me better, at least for now.

A rather nightmarish attempted return trip here, with ice reported on the runways at Orly and the whole crowded BOAC planeload of people getting on and off the aircraft and back and forth through customs three or four times before the airline canceled the flight and grudgingly lodged us passengers in a hotel, after a dogged if gentlemanly protest on our behalf by an engaging Oxonian named Totten, who teaches in an English school in Paris.

In compliance with the British laws of that time, we had exchanged all our English money for francs or dollars or pesetas or something else, and by the time the flight was definitely canceled, the money-changers had closed up. We had no English cash to pay for lodgings, and international credit cards did not yet exist for the general public.

Against our disgruntlement—I remember one pudgy Italian with a wife and two babies who shouted and waved his arms—the counterman merely indicated that he was sorry, but under company regulations we were on our own. Totten had friends in London and plenty of places to stay, but he took up our cause and staged an understated little drama of British class distinction. In a definitely "U" accent, with quiet courtesy, he demanded to speak to someone more highly placed, and when that someone and the next, still with a touch of cockney or the provinces in their speech, proved to be as rule-bound as the counterman about our plight, Totten managed finally to make them produce an admirably groomed and well-spoken gentleman in a sort of commodore's uniform, with a little dark goatee.

U toe-to-toe with U, Totten outlined our problem to this person, who listened carefully.

The commodore said at last, "Well, it *is* against our policies, but I see your point. If you were to insist, I'm afraid I should have to agree."

Totten replied, "Well, I'm afraid I do insist."

So we were all put up in a nearby hotel.

JAN. 5: Then on to Paris in the morning. The lovely bright Englishwoman aboard who stuck with me and Totten, a good-humored threesome. There were sparks between me and her, but she told me she had a "special person" in Paris and when we got here she was welcomed warmly by a very plain American PFC in uniform, undistinguished in appearance or speech. Love being, as they say, like the dew, which falls as easily upon the horse turd as upon the rose. Not that I am all that much of a rose . . .

Jacques is marrying his Marthe tomorrow. He is harried and full of doubts, but Marthe is not. . . .

JAN. 6: Recently read: Ford Madox Ford, *It Was the Nightingale*. Memoirs, in his back-and-forth way, from about World War One to the mid-thirties. A civilized mind, acceptably inconsistent, contradicting himself all the way through and not worrying about it. Also glanced through his *Great Trade Route* and a book he did on France, and another on English villages. Quite a fellow.

Ford Madox Ford . . . Sam Hynes was doing some scholarly work on this author, and it was probably at his place in London that I had found these books. I especially admired Ford's World War One tetralogy *Parade's End,* to which I had also been introduced by Sam some years earlier. In fact, I admired it so much that the novel I started writing the following year, *A Speckled Horse,* was heavily infected with Fordian mannerisms, and in the long run, despite my continued great respect for his best work, I came to see this as a major flaw, stylistic imitation leading nearly always to awkwardness.

Digested styles of others are another matter; through your reading they sink into your unconscious and when they emerge in your writing at some point, they belong to you for better or worse. I believe that nearly all worthwhile writing is flavored by its author's reading, and the more reading he does, the better. But I had not fully digested Ford while writing that faulty novel.

JAN. 7: Graham Greene, *This Gun for Hire.* A pure thriller, nicely told as always with Greene. The most notable difference between these and his serious novels is flat, fast characterization and little probing. But both the thrillers and the serious ones have the same end effect of bleakness, grayness, sadness, emptiness, Greene's view of the world, which I accept but cannot share. J. W. Hills, *A Summer on the Test.* A quiet, civilized fishing book, enjoyable and very dry-fly. But for the moment anyhow I think I have lost most of that tense and highly technical absorption. Much of the time I would just as soon fish with nymphs though not, by preference, streamers.

Hemingway, *For Whom the Bell Tolls.* About my fourth reading, and it seems as good as before if not better after learning a little about Spain at first hand. You think of him as having

been sucked left but he wasn't really, at least not in the sense
of being taken in. He did know Spain and Spaniards and
also knew the point at which he couldn't know them, and
admitted that. The love material may be, as practically always
with him, a little too ideal, but he does mean love and not
just acrobatics in bed. The war parts are good, and the friendships, and the Spaniards, and the feel. As always H. is a little
discouraging to me with his enormous capacity for living and
seeing.

Most literate adult Spaniards on the Peninsula in those days,
being conservative survivors of the Civil War period, seemed to
look on Hemingway as a radical Red, except those who liked
bullfights and tended to view him more leniently. Gustavo Morales, a conservative but not unreasonable person, once said to me
flatly and with force that *For Whom the Bell Tolls* was an anti-
Spanish book. . . .

Hemingway, incidentally, did not much like Ford Madox
Ford, despite the boosts Ford gave him when he was getting
started, in terms of jobs and printed praise. In his later reminis-
cence of his early days in Paris, *A Moveable Feast,* Hemingway
included a bitterly scurrilous portrait of Ford. This fitted in, of
course, with his abandonment of other benefactors like Sher-
wood Anderson and Gertrude Stein, but since he admired good
writing—and the best of Ford is beautiful—I have always wondered about the roots of this antipathy. And recently, in a book of
Hemingway's letters, I think I found an answer: The reason for
his dislike of Ford was chiefly commercial. The young Ernest
was a bit paranoid about money, and he came to believe that
Ford, as founder of *The Transatlantic Review,* was unfairly stingy
with the authors who submitted work for publication, and in
business dealings with others.

Maybe Ford really was close-fisted, for he himself was often
short of cash. But it does seem a pity that two such figures did not
mesh and become good friends.

JAN. 8: Paris is dull this time, no accessible people worth talking to, no women, no work, no nothing. It is coming to me strongly that I don't really fit in over here. Of people I've met I have truly liked and communicated with only a few—Cochrane (though he's more and more a problem), Pepe, Lena, the Brooks, and maybe three or four others. Have found no group into which I want to fit, but for that matter have not found one elsewhere either, not since the youthful brotherhoods of college and the Marine Corps.

There is no notation in the journal of my first Madrid meeting with Alexander Brook and his wife Gina (hard "g"), mentioned above, but they became friends who mattered a great deal to me. They were both painters, then in their fifties, and in his younger years Alex had made a considerable splash in the American art world, winning a Carnegie prize back in the 1930s. Since then he had been pretty much eclipsed by the Abstract Expressionists and such, and had been doing mainly portraits, though distinctive ones that were much sought after. Lame from polio in childhood, he was the son of Russian immigrants (he said Brook was their actual name as written down at Ellis Island, though in Russian it was probably spelled Vryk or something like that in Cyrillic letters), an intelligent, moody, often irascible or bitter man. Gina was vague and lovely and highly intuitive, and we three liked one another from the start. I had been given their name by Jan Kuhn, and when I telephoned they had thought I would be homosexual, for that was the kind of young men she usually sent around. . . .

We did things together, I serving as interpreter when needed. Nearly every Sunday morning, for instance, Alex and I would go to the huge Madrid flea market, the Rastro, where his sharp eye could pick out treasures like rolled-up good primitive paintings or walking sticks with intricate handles of ivory or silver or brass that interested him because of his lifelong lameness. In their car we explored outward from the city, and near one ancient mountain pueblo, Chinchón, there was a small medieval castle for sale cheap which Alex was tempted to buy, but didn't. In a sense the shape of my future was determined by this friendship, for it was through the Brooks, three or four years later, that I met Jane Cole, my present wife and the mother of my daughters.

JAN. 10, STILL PARIS AND TIRED OF IT: New Yearish resolutions: get to know the Tony type better [Tony Stubbing, a British artist met through the Brooks]; send for the heavy fly rod to use on salmon; make a hotel reservation for San Fermín; plan some excursions with the Brooks; look for an apartment; see about horses; check on literary societies in Madrid; make a list of "must" Spanish reading; make a vocabulary list and go carefully through the grammar book again; make application for the Galician salmon fishing or talk to Tavo Morales about Asturias; Spanish music and dance; British Institute.

A Mexican movie I saw last night, *La Red,* which got the Cannes prize for storytelling by pictures. A compendium of all the defects of Latin overdramatization—much soul-staring, much unmeaningful violence, much heavily groaning sex. For me the scenery was the only thing in it worth a damn. It would take a Frenchman to give it a prize, partly for the tits and partly because the locale is so far away as to make impossible things seem possible.

Am somehow at the moment, probably unfairly, a bit fed up with the more flamboyant manifestations of the Latin temperament, mainly as exemplified in French arties and bohemians. Maybe the stay in England among the phlegmatic cousins started this. These people seem ephemeral and it is hard to take seriously their loves and hates and enthusiasms since in another hour (one feels, unfairly) they will have finished their dance and will have bred beneath the willows and fallen into the stream to be eaten by trout. I feel a little of this with all people who are not what the Spanish call gente seria, but especially with the more emotional types of Frenchmen.

I still need a *status*. Not prestige, but just a good solid spot in the social morass on which to plant myself and from which to deal with other people. We all need touchstones for one another. To gain my own touchstone, I need to write a BOOK.

JAN. 11: A small room in a small grubby hotel not far from St. Germain des Prés. Plush curtains and bedspread, dark green and heavy as Hudson's Bay blankets, a shallow armoire into which my jackets will not fit without slanting them, a washbasin that retches and gurgles all night and morning when other people drain their own basins or piss into them, and a big leaky window looking out onto the largest and loudest market on the Left Bank. This sort of thing is fine and romantic when you're in your early twenties, but when you pass thirty it's not worth a damn.

A movie yesterday, Alec Guinness in *The Captain's Paradise*. A rather strained piece of work, for him, and some of it embarrassing, as when he dances the jitterbug. Reflects with a good deal of humor the British attitude toward lesser breeds. A jarring note was the extremely bad Spanish spoken by the people in it who were supposed to be Spanish. Another, *Stalag 17*. Am a hell of a moviegoer lately, but have had little else to do while waiting for the trip back to Madrid. This one is like many war novels and films, though it has fewer stock characters and is funny as hell. We Americans tend to be at our best in war, but probably all other people are too. At their best and at their worst.

Mary G.: She had dyed blonde hair and long horse cheeks (the Spanish called her unkindly La Caballona) and a married daughter back at home in England. Her Mayfair accent, insofar as a Texan was qualified to judge, was impeccable and her manners queenly even when she was drinking, which was more or less steadily during waking hours. Once after a Mallorcan barroom riot in which my chief role had been that of would-be peacemaker, she had told people that I had hit her. Even later, after I had apologized for what I had not done, she kept on believing it, amicably. The uproar had started out as Americans vs. Britons, and I think the one who actually socked her, by pure accident, had been a young soldier named McHugh, a good fellow on leave from Germany, who entered the fighting when he heard derogatory words about Americans. In consonance with the irrationality of the affair, he ended up getting knocked across the barroom by my large friend Robert Cochrane, who was also very American and who had started the whole God-damned mess.

One thing that perhaps keeps us Americans from being as often pompous as Europeans is that during the natural period for the onset of pomposity, at around college age, we are still considered children and are not taken seriously. So we usually get over it. Here where adulthood is frequently forced on them at seventeen or eighteen, the stiff know-it-allness tends to get cemented. I am thinking of Jean-Marie's brother Antoine.

JAN. 21, MADRID: Back here and glad of it. But back also into the Spanish confusion and mindlessness and personalness of all relationships. It is good to see the Brooks. Their friends Charles and Lael Wertenbaker, who are Virginians, and we talked about the problems and advantages of being Southern. Cochrane due to show up here again soon and I am not eager for that moral and time-consuming load.

I seem not to have recorded that second visit of friend Cochrane to Madrid, but I think it was much like the first one. He still wanted guidance and I had little to give, except to say again that he ought to go home. He did so not long thereafter, and later, in a letter from his Lambie Chuck that I received in the Canaries, I was shocked to learn that after getting back to New York he had walked down a subway track to meet an oncoming train. It did not kill him but tore him up badly. Years later Kicker B., one of the Yalies I had gone to Pamplona with, who had been fascinated by Cochrane in Palma, told me of running into him in a New York bar. He said Cochrane was as funny as he had ever been, even crippled permanently as he was. . . .

Pepe Mut was in Madrid by then and we saw a good bit of each other, browsing supper together at various tascas with their special tidbits, having coffee at a café later, and then walking the dimly lit streets, sometimes for hours, talking and arguing and telling jokes. The English-language program in which he was studying was run by American academics, a couple of whom I had known at the University of Texas during my teaching days there. We got together with them sometimes, and one evening in a hotel suite with three or four Spaniards and three or four Americans present, the conversation was in Spanish and one of the academics secretly started a tape recorder. When he played the tape back to us later I listened to my own voice with surprise and some chagrin. I was very fluent by then, more so than the academics, but my vowels and diphthongs were still pure West Texas.

This made a notable dent in my impression of myself as an increasingly international sort of fellow, and was probably salutary.

JAN. 23: A book that sister Nancy sent from Texas: J. H. Allen, *Southwest.* Absolutely beautiful in the beginning—have never seen better Texas writing. Then it goes to pieces in overpoetic utterance and alcoholic self-dramatization and stories about potheads, a lost Toltec capital, etc. Is there something about that region that makes us break down like that?

Why are women necessary? Without their pull I could live happily and austerely in a mountainside cabin somewhere. And

I haven't seen one in a long time that I would want to marry, not one. Not even other people's wives. Mariví is at least good for clear thinking on my part on this subject, relieving the pressure as she does.

She was a volatile, wacky Canary Islands high-grade professional with whom I became briefly involved, and she was living in the hotel against all of Tavo Morales's precepts, maybe because she had charmed him. And yes, she was indeed charming.

JAN. 24: Mariví, and the good Spanish whores in general, not that there aren't better ones than she in terms of temperament. They are different from their sisters elsewhere in my opinion, certainly less gross than the American and Mexican types I have been around and was never attracted to. Most of them came to the capital from pueblos as maidservants, then got involved with the horny eldest son or the father and were fired. They would be doing something else if the system permitted. Mariví in America by now, with her looks and crazy vivacity, would have been married to money two or three times and would be living happily and well off the proceeds, which seems little more honorable of course than what she is doing here.

With Pepe last night and two other Spanish officers, very pleasantly making the rounds of the tascas drinking white wine and eating the varied tidbits of shellfish and pork and such, called tapas, that are the specialties of different places. They have hardly any money but you have to argue them into letting you pay for anything. Have finished a first draft of the Swedish-girl story, but am not feeling much satisfaction about it. A book, a book, a book is what I need to write.

JAN. 25: Reading this a.m. of Hemingway's death [a mistaken report as it turned out; he later walked out alive from an African plane crash], while having coffee and churros in the Cafetería Puerto Rico on the Gran Vía. Students in a mass passed by on the sidewalk demonstrating loudly for "Gi-bral-tar! Es-pañ-ol! Gi-bral-tar! Es-pañ-ol!" in support of General Franco's current campaign to get that strongpoint back from the British. They might as well be Communists for all the thoughts they have in their heads. At any rate Hemingway died in his own way and God rest him and bless him for having existed, with all his personal shortcomings.

Pepe telling of being a young foot soldier in the Nationalist ranks at Guadalajara where Mussolini's crack troops and armor and airplanes first came to Franco's aid, and of the great pride he and his fellows felt when the enemy Reds across the way stopped the Italians cold and sent the terrified survivors stampeding backward: "We laughed!" he said. "Es que eran *españoles,* joder! Tenían *cojones!*" They were *Spaniards,* with *balls!*

That was where the miners from Asturias and Guipúzcoa had strapped dynamite around their waists and jumped up on the Italian tanks and blown them up along with themselves, and I am sure this tale was something that Pepe told me in private, for his fellow officers and indeed most other Establishment Spaniards of that time had very little flexibility in their view of the Civil War and the Republican Reds. However, neither he nor I was especially rigid about politics. Young and from a conservative and Catholic background, he had enlisted for Franco at seventeen, and was still quietly proud of having done so, but he had an ability to see things whole, which was part of the reason I liked him as much as I did. He viewed blue-shirt Falangists caustically, telling sharp-edged jokes about them, and could be funny too about the titled Spanish aristocracy and their pretensions.

Another Civil War tale he once told me, grimly humorous, involved a Nationalist politician named Muñoz Seca, who had been imprisoned by the Republicans and was taken from his cell one day to face a firing squad. They asked if he had any last words, and he said that yes he did.

"Gentlemen," he said, "you can take my freedom. You can take my house and my money and my family and at last my life. But there is one thing you will never be able to take away from me."

He paused, and they asked him what this thing was.

He said, "You will never, never, in this world or any other world, be able to take away from me this enormous, this stupendous fear that I have of you!"

On matters involving politics Pepe tended to be mildly rightist, which didn't bother me; I had grown up among much more emphatic conservatives and in fact was myself in many ways no dogged liberal. On occasions when he fulminated a bit, I often agreed with him. Once a fellow named Tilton, an early hippie type living in Paris, came to Madrid on a visit and looked me up at the behest of some mutual friend in New York. We rather disliked each other on sight, I in the coat and tie I usually wore in that city, he bushy-haired and bearded and dressed in a T-shirt and stained jeans into the waistband of which he deeply tucked his hands—a more or less standard getup now but glaringly distinctive back then, especially in Spain.

Pepe happened to come around when Tilton and I were talking at the hotel, and had very little to say until after the bearded one had left.

"Por dios, hombre, qué *animal!*" he then said. "Qué *marica!* And what is he doing with his fingers down there, playing with his balls?"

JAN. 27: Watching TV makes you feel afterward as though you had been playing with yourself. Is America destined to become a nation of mental masturbators?

Last night I saw the Quintero Brothers' *Malvaloca* with Amparo Rivelles. The play itself on reflection was pretty much of a tearjerker and was badly twisted to provide a happy ending. But she is wonderful, a pure andaluza.

JAN. 28: Talking with Alex Brook last night. The deep sadness he feels as a result of aging and of the age itself, being démodé and evidently having lost confidence in his art. A fine man, but what a weak hold all artists and writers have upon solidity. His daughter is divorcing back in the States, and his money is running out.

[Things weren't really all that bad, but Alex had a Russian gift for sinking into the depths and pulling you down there with him, reminding me often of my ex-wife Bryan during the time of our marriage.]

FEB. 2: Have been thinking a lot about the Spanish and their war and the society they have. This has been sparked in part by reading Foltz, *The Masquerade in Spain,* which is straight un-Red reporting and rather devastating. His theory of The Family which is behind all the regimes and continues in power. Most of it seems right. Pepe's friend the other night—intense, hating England, his pupils contracting to dots when he spoke of the Civil War and the Reds.

I have an article organized but unwritten on a "U.S. Go Home" theme. *The New Yorker*'s letter of rejection about the "Alley" story, forwarded by Schaffner, rather hurt, because it is true.

FEB. 8: Politics. Anybody with sense cares about it, but you either fit into one of the organized systems, or you don't. If you can't manage partisan enthusiasm and you see advantages and disadvantages in all or most of the sides, I guess what you do is shut up and try to quit thinking about the matter.

Old John: This statement was all right in its way, but it could only have issued from an esthetically minded native of a privileged country like the United States. The lives of people of many other nationalities are crucially and often mortally affected by the political forces that swirl around them. Even we Americans did not then and do not now have the option of ignoring the influence of politics on our lives.

Nevertheless, in terms of my work, I have tended to regard partisan uproar and the polemics it engenders as pretty irrelevant. On the few occasions when I have engaged in preachment, nearly always in defense of the natural world, I have had the feeling that however honest and expressive the writing might be, it had no chance of permanence. If your cause won, great, but the writing's work was then done and it sank down into limbo. If the cause lost, the same thing happened. Only polemicists with the genius of people like Swift and Milton could hope for more; their lingering potent appeal is based not on the causes they espoused but on their verbal, narrative, and dramatic magnificence.

Yes, to hope for lastingness in one's work is an arrogance. Yet one does hope for it; improbable though it may be. . . .

Maybe a little of this antipathy toward politics trickled down from my Confederate forebears, whose political framework crumpled at Appomattox. But in the main, I believe, it derived from my ineradicable pessimism about human directions— which was always mitigated, however, by a joy in being alive in a time when there were still so many good people to know, so many meaningful books to read, so many fine things to do. . . .

FEB. 9: One tries to get into literature by circling the high chain-link fence and looking for holes. It is a hell of a long walk and they've got a very good maintenance crew on that fence. I seem to have walked around the son of a bitch about fifteen times now. Which is as it should be. Instead of walking, *run*.

To a stage revue with Otto Meyer [the Bavarian ex–German embassy guardsman who was manager of the Luxor] and Tavo Morales. On my own I have seen only revistas folklóricas. This one was surprisingly professional, with good comics and a big bosomy deep-voiced Argentine singer who was all woman.

Cojones: Some have got them and make the most of them, some ain't got 'em and make the most of that. There is room for both types, as witness Ernest Hemingway and John Randolph. Most of us with average sets of balls mosey along in between, feeling masculine around the one sort and vaguely inadequate around the other. When you see a woman like that Argentine last night, you feel that you'd like to have a pair, as Paco Alarcón said, like houses.

Randolph was a quirky, testy, brilliant Virginia aristocrat of the late eighteenth and early nineteenth centuries, whose pronounced effeminacy a coarse fellow-congressman once dwelt upon scornfully in public debate, with references to his own virility.

Randolph replied, "In the faculty of which you boast, sir, a slave is your equal and a donkey your infinite superior!"

MARCH 9, TORREMOLINOS: On the move again, urged by the periodic restlessness and facilitated by the departure from Madrid of Eva Flores.

Evita was a fiery and virginal little Cuban singer who had been staying at the Luxor during a nightclub engagement, and who fascinated me. She traveled with her "mother," who I am sure was only an elderly maidservant, but all the female performers who wanted to avoid entanglements and insistently amorous Spaniards did that. She had spent a lot of time in Argentina and had a rather strong zhuh-zhah accent when speaking, though when she sang her tropical songs her accent was pure Cuban, and she was very very good, earning about $1,000 a week even in Spain at that time. Me she regarded wryly as her "intellectual" friend and not as anything else, to my disgruntlement. Tough as a boot in some ways from surviving the Latin show world's pitfalls, she was quite innocent in others. Once when I took her to the Prado and told her stories about the painters as we looked at their pictures, she got upset and angry over the immorality of it all, especially over the relationship between Goya and his Maja Desnuda, the Duchess of Alba. As I told her about that painting's reputed background, she gazed at it and then turned to me with a frown.

"I don't like all that!" she said.

I said it was just the way people were, or had been.

"Tú te estás poniendo muy pesado, Juanito," she said. You're getting very heavy. . . .

At any rate, she did leave Spain for wherever her next engagement was, silent "mother" in tow. Once, in a moment of confidence, she had told me she was saving herself for a very rich husband, and I hope she found him.

MARCH 11, TORREMOLINOS: Reading Madariaga, *Englishmen, Frenchmen, Spaniards,* there being a considerable if heterogeneous library here at the hotel, made up of books from some British center that existed in Málaga before the Civil War. Am utterly alone in a place that seems at first glance to be a great deal more full of Englishmen than it probably is. A bright room with birdsong outside and the cool air full of sun, old Spanish Army biplanes flying, and no one I know to fill the time with. Have finished the "U.S. Go Home" article, but don't much like it.

Andalucía and its poor persistent bastards around railroad and bus stations and airline terminals, touting hotels or excursions or grabbing at your luggage. The first thing I did in Málaga was to lose my temper at one, then feel ashamed. They force it. There are none here, though. Once you have your bags stashed somewhere and get the traveling look off of your face, they leave you alone.

MARCH 12: It is working. In the aloneness I am forced to consider myself, which if not a very edifying process, may bring some results. Am dreaming at night too, always a good sign with me.

Reading Negley Farson, *The Story of a Lake,* a rambling chaotic thing in which he incorporates as fiction, though without fictionalizing it enough, much of the material of his better, autobiographical *The Way of a Transgressor.* It is less effective here but somehow more intimate because of the fictional pose—the frigid wife, the love of bitches, the alcoholism, etc. A sympathetic figure, full of life and loving it, yet with hatred of much of it too, like me—America's betrayal of its promise through the rape of the wilderness, the sterility of life in general there. I feel kinship, but this man differs in that he had *done* things and *been* somebody. His defeat was therefore meaningful and had a certain power. Yours, if you let it happen, won't be.

At least I can write better than Farson can, but I'd better demonstrate that in published print.

Other people's nasty children are slightly more bearable when you don't speak the language they are complaining in. [The children in question were Danish.]

In Madariaga, I am struck by the similarity of French views as he defines them, and New York Jewish views, both being based on logic.

MARCH 14: The way I talk my head off to sympathetic people found while traveling. It would be better if that came out in my writing, though often the talking does seem to clarify things. These Moroneys are pleasant people, the better kind of Americans. [He was an Oregon plywood manufacturer and she was his second wife, a very bright lady.]

It seems the *Holiday* article raised a slight tidal wave in Palma's foreign set, and I still feel a little guilty. The hell with it.

MARCH 19: A trip to Ronda with the Moroneys yesterday was all that it was supposed to be, a bit stunning in truth. An enthusiastic kid guide with all of his information garbled. The wide and famous old plaza de toros where the Romeros fought huge five-year-old bulls long, long ago, with a movie screen defining its present function. Modern toreros quit fighting there because out in the middle they were too far from refuge. . . . Whitewashed villages scattered up the mountainsides, and on the sterile heights the crude shelters of desperately poor people built of random slabs of native marble ("I dreamt I dwelt in marble halls," said Mrs. Moroney), and seeing Gibraltar from up there. A special woman, Mrs. M., and I wish I could find one like her my own age or younger.

MARCH 20: W. B. Pemberton's *William Cobbett,* a readable account of a man I had hitherto known only through oblique references. A fine, noisy, powerful, eighteenth-century person-ality fighting mainly against the selling out of "Old England" to the forces of the Industrial Revolution. It was too late even then, that fight, though some of us are still carrying it on in our own stupid ways. His ideal is what Jefferson believed in and thought possible, a society of sturdy hard-working self-respecting yeomen, and what F. M. Ford with clear eyes was mourning for, and what most men nowadays have no concep-tion of, so that it is impossible. Spain might be able to have some of it even now if the upper classes were worthy of the people, but they're not.

It is queer how I suddenly get sated with individuals, even good ones. Moroney, for instance—such intense naïveté finally gets quite wearing. The way he got into a political argument with this Falangist type González, after saying in preface that he knew he shouldn't talk about politics in Spain. Hell no he shouldn't, not him. . . .

MARCH 23, ALGECIRAS: With a bitch of a cold, red-eyed as a hog. Torremolinos shaped up rather nicely toward the end, with good people—the one-armed South African, June the pantomime artist, the two Ohio girls who became good friends of mine. I was able to help linguistically when one of them developed appendicitis and was deathly (and rightly) scared of the local Spanish medical setup, and we finally got her to Gibraltar, just across the bay from where I am now.

Still feeling a bit guilty about the Palma article, and that leads to the old basic question of whether writing, which is so often a betrayal of relationships and confidences, is actually an honorable profession.

The older English in this place, my God. Mainly aged rheumatics and lungers, staying here because it's far from the British climate but close to Gib. The canes, the coughs (hoo, hoo, hoo—gently so as not to hemorrhage), the faces drawn into lines of fury by pain. The Hotel Reina Victoria, aptly named.

MARCH 28, SEVILLA: Went from Algeciras to Tangiers with the Moroneys, of whom (him at least) I had finally grown tired. He is full of nerves and totally unsuited for travel, unconscious of his own rubbernecking and innocence. (*Can* you be conscious of innocence?) His excitement when I pointed out an actual pimp at work. . . . They drove on down into Morocco, and I wandered around Tetuán a little, then with luck caught a plane to here. It is a relief to be on my own again.

Am contemplating a cheap lone return train trip to Madrid via little-frequented places like Cáceres, Badajoz, etc. Probably would be a little rough but I might see something. Would like some agreeable company, but I think it's best to be alone now, forced to face myself and think.

Read yesterday García Lorca's *Yerma,* about a childless woman. It gave me twinges in remembrance of Bryan, also of Lena. A letter from Mrs. Pemberton [the admiral's wife] gave me a better feeling about the expatriate piece, for she is a very sharp lady and agrees with all I said in it. Also a fan letter from a girl in Japan.

MARCH 30: Saw the Varners last night. [I had known him in the English department in Austin; his main work was on Garcilaso de la Vega "El Inca" and he was doing research now in the old colonial archives in Seville.] He is an odd Texan-scholar mixture of the rough-hewn and the bookish, which is all to the good if not entirely homogeneous. Many martinis with them, and I dreamed wildly all night long—those weird authorial dreams where you are both participant and creator, directing the action. In one I was sailing along a shallow, rocky, golden, ominous coastline like that deserted shore en route to La Fossa.

Afternoon, after sleep. Sometimes this guilt, over the bad things I have done and the good ones I have not (shades of my Calvinist forebears), nearly chokes me. How long will I be able to stand that? A sane and sardonic answer would be, not too long, and maybe eventually you'll actually get something done on account of it, you sad bastard.

A long journal passage here details the character and background of a proposed protagonist in a novel, very much like the protagonist of the novel that seized me later on, in the Canaries, and became my faulty unpublished opus *A Speckled Horse*. Very much like myself, too, with the addition of crippling head wounds like those a roommate of mine at the Long Beach naval hospital had suffered at Tarawa.

Obviously that book was destined to be a "bildungsroman" in the time-bruised tradition of Goethe, the tale of a young man's tribulations along his road toward self-realization, and the more tribulations the better. But at least I was thinking more and more now about honest writing, and had abandoned the "one for me and one for them" approach that had kept me financially afloat for a time. I believe that the "Corporal" short story referred to earlier in this memoir was one of the last of my slick efforts; I don't remember its content or what happened to it, nor do I care.

Magazine articles were different, being primarily journalism. You could write them accurately and honestly without too much fretting over esthetics, and the payment you received for them had none of the dirty feel that the slicks' money, for me at least, had always seemed to have.

APRIL 1, MÉRIDA: I missed the only daytime train north, so I think I may wait till evening and go directly to Madrid, an all-night ride. Will catch Salamanca another time. Mérida is a pleasant backwater with a fairly prosperous (for Spain) look to it. Its people do not stare at you or bother you. I have seen little here but the Roman theater and amphitheater. Thoughts in the latter place: Here the governor, a little bored so far from Rome where things really counted, or maybe stupid-provincial-vain with his local power, or maybe just serenely supreme—here he put the old thumb down on many a miserable African or Christian who had come blinking up out of the tunnels to face whatever there was to face. Just as today the alcalde or the president of the local Falange or whoever, in the plaza de toros a quarter-mile away, gives his consent for the faena to begin.

There is a stork's nest on the cupola outside my window, with a stork in it.

Spanish hunting: He had done it once, a cacería on the estate of a Falangist marqués to which he had been invited through friendship with a businessman in Madrid, the marqués's cousin. It had been nice shooting, the partridges rocketing over from the far-off line of peasant beaters, and in downing twenty-three birds he had done better than most of the forty or so people who had taken part, even with a mismatched pair of borrowed guns. But it had left a dirty taste afterward, being too easy, too patrician, too organized. Fundamentally he did not like any

kind of shooting that was bigger than two or three men and a
dog, or two men at a water tank when the doves came flitting
in fast and low in the evening, and a lot of walking so that you
were nicely bushed afterward, and your one good gun that you
carried and loaded yourself, and cleaning your own birds afterward. This other way seemed wrong, as when you had watched
oilmen on the King Ranch hunting deer from comfortable
chairs riveted to the tops of Buicks. Afterward in the marqués's
large, thick-walled, whitewashed country house, with a big fire
going and everybody full of good food, they had not talked
about shooting but about politics, vehemently. They grew more
vehement with the brandy and in the presence of a foreigner,
and they had not been happy over his silence. What they
wanted was his agreement or his absence. Well, you could find
that in Texas too.

Bullfights—he hardly ever missed one any more if it was
held anywhere he could get to. It was mostly lousy rotten now,
cheating and arranged and scared, without nobility, and even
the caste of the bulls was going fast. And when you saw the
four or five decent things that you saw in maybe six or eight
corridas, you knew you were seeing something that would not
exist at all in another few years.

APRIL 4, MADRID: Back here rather empty of soul and with
no idea of how to refill the son of a bitch, they not yet having
furnished service stations for that. Outside of psychiatrists,
whom I distrust, besides being nervous around most of their
cured ones, who carry themselves through life like crystal.

Have begun to play with fishing tackle again. . . .

APRIL 5: A thought for today—most people who have a great
desire to be left alone, and then try it, find that no one much
was bothering them in the first place, just they themselves,
and that, alone, they bother themselves more than ever.

[Juan Ramón Jiménez, in one of his "Maxims" that I read later on, says, "En la soledad no se encuentra más que lo que se lleva a ella." In solitude you find only what you take there with you. . . .]

The really empty types at Brooks' yesterday, this East Coast patrician Tony and Emily Henshall pair, former portrait-clients of Alex's. Actually the man is upper-crust British of the purely decorative sort. I guess they represent the true international set, with lots of money (she, anyhow), but if so I feel no envy. He did have some funny stories about his pansy brother and his ill-natured old titled father in England.

APRIL 8: Yesterday at Tony Stubbing's home in the slums, all sort of easygoing and sloppy and full of arty activity. The young Spanish dancer sister-in-law and her friends shaping pots, and the great new kiln they have built that may or may not work when fired. Hawking lures and fishing tackle and playing the guitar and all very vital and honest.

And in huge contrast last night a visit to Mr. Desmond Walton's exquisite apartment, with much supercilious conversation as African masks and pornographic pictures stared down from the walls, and Mike Cooper, who had gone there with me, wouldn't say anything and afterward was practically ill. Me too. Walton's painful boyfriend showing off his knowledge of Spain and telling about gypsies who would jerk you off for eight pesetas, and about his own attempt at bullfighting, occasionally breaking into Spanish for a quite poor dirty joke at which Walton laughed heartily.

Desmond Walton was a retired American diplomat, effeminate but cultivated and highly intelligent, and I had liked him till that night. Mike Cooper was a frail, decent, shy young man I had known in Palma, a sort of lost soul but a thoughtful and sensitive one. He had been making a minimal living in New York as a commercial artist, turning out things like newspaper ads and lurid paperback book covers while envisioning more noble efforts. Saving up enough money to get himself across the Atlantic and to the island, he had stayed at a little distance from the expatriate crowd and had set about painting street and maritime scenes, working toward a style that would be entirely his own. This aspiration was close enough to my own that we recognized kinship and got to know each other.

But his personal style did not evolve very fast if at all, and then his money ran out. At this point one of the tough middle-aged American widows or divorcées living there, a solid, ewe-faced woman named Ethel, who had expressed interest in his work and had even bought a picture or two, suggested that he move into her house and do his painting there. This invitation turned out to have strings attached, and before long Mike was a kept man, miserable not only because his work was going poorly but because of his shameful status.

Now, in Madrid, he had escaped from Ethel and was headed back home to New York, where he expected without joy to resume his work on sexy, violent, and lurid paperback covers. . . .

Tony Stubbing, on the other hand, was about as far as a man could get from being a lost soul. He was a fascinating figure to me and we became rather close friends in the long run, but maverick though he was he had a wall of British reserve that never quite broke down. In part also, this derived from a need in him to deal with other people at arm's length, something I'll comment on later. He came from an upper-class background and had the self-assurance conferred by that, had been one of Marshal Montgomery's young courier aides during the war, kept a kestrel on a perch beside his easel, could fly a plane, caught surprising numbers of trout by dapping stealthily with a twelve-foot bamboo fly rod, handled horses beautifully, was the best shot I've ever known with a catapult, etc., etc., etc. He signed his name on most of his paintings and elsewhere as N. H. Stubbing, the "N" standing for Newton, from which "Tony" had been derived.

He was married to a mettlesome girl named Rosa María, usually rendered Rosemary, whose Spanish father had been a college professor in Germany and whose mother was German, and they lived in a poor district of Madrid on a street called Cuesta de las Descargas, which Tony said meant Shit Hill, though it didn't quite. He had a full beard (rare then, and much rarer in Spain), wore loose baggy tweeds, and spoke absolutely fluent Spanish with an abominable (cultivated, I think) strong English accent. Through family connections he had a subsistence job as night watchman at the British embassy, where I used to go visit him sometimes and we would sit out back under the dark night sky, talking and tending the fire in the big brick pottery kiln he had built against the embassy wall.

He had wonderful tales, Tony, some from his youth in the south of England where an old gypsy poacher had taught him many sly country tricks relating to fish and game, a few stories from the war, and more from the years afterward when he had done much wandering. He had fallen out with his parents, wanted only to paint, and had been broke in a number of different places. One winter night in Paris he didn't even have enough money for a flophouse bed, so in order to stay warm he walked the empty streets for many hours. At around four o'clock, in a dim narrow byway somewhere near the Porte d'Orléans, he suddenly saw the pavement just ahead come alive, grayly and lumpily swarming at him, chittering. Running back from this apparition, he scaled a lamppost and hung from its crossbar while rats passed solidly below, an army stretching from wall to wall of the street and fifty yards long.

A gendarme later told him they had been changing sewers. After cleaning one out they moved massively at night to another, starved and savage. It was not good to be caught by them; the gendarme himself had seen a raw human skeleton after such an occurrence, or at least he said he had.

Tony will recur in these pages, and a few years back he turned up at our country place in Texas on his way to California with a new and American wife, but later died on Long Island, a respected artist by then.

APRIL 10: Reading Charles Wertenbaker, the fellow I met at the Brooks', *Death of Kings,* an intensive liberal examination of conscience, of the generation of the thirties and what has happened to it, all of this reflected in the workings of Time-Life Inc., where Wertenbaker was once a big wheel before quitting. It is an intelligent tract rather than the novel it purports to be, not writing in my ideal sense, but I do have much respect for him as a person after reading it.

APRIL 14, CANGAS DE ONÍS, ASTURIAS: [This was the trip I made with Tavo Morales to his home territory on the Cantabrian coast.] Don't really like visiting even partly like this. The Spanish are too hospitable and there is much sense of obligation. All these people flocking down on the poor damned salmon, or maybe I'm just pissed off because I have caught no fish and have had no time to read and think. But it is very hard-fished water, peasants out with worms etc.

APRIL 15, SAME: Another bad day on the fishing but nice—cold, but with plenty of exercise. Nobody else caught much either. Beautiful country, classic—neat, solid villages, huge chestnut trees, good-looking peasants, wild mountains, clean water, everything green and budding and blossoming with spring. The ground is strewn with a number of kinds of flowers as in that old tapestry of the Unicorn Hunt. No other Americans or indeed anybody but Spaniards around. Tonight to a chigre with a lagar in back. . . .

APRIL 20, MADRID: It turned out fine in the end, hardly any salmon caught (none by me) but there were good people and glorious country and finally a binge in a cider mill at Gijón, the lagar mentioned above, where I ended up crawling into a huge chestnut-wood barrel's cleaning port and singing hillbilly songs with my head sticking out. My audience was drunk enough to be appreciative, but they liked even better (I did too) the lovely jotas asturianas sung by young workers, male and female, who were bottling cider as we watched. The hangover I had the next day was special, augmented by the laxative effect of that beverage. Many stories, Civil War and otherwise. Then back in Tavo Morales's car through the high pass at Pajares and down into bare León and through Valladolid and the Guadarrama and here. Brought back big centollo spider crabs and lobsters to the Brooks, in lieu of a salmon.

Tavo served during the Civil War with a Basque unit from Navarra, that mountain Carlist and ultra-Catholic stronghold which went with Franco, while the coastal vascos mainly stuck with the Republic, a traumatic split because Basques in general like their fellow Basques more than they like other kinds of people. One morning when they knew there were Red Basques in the lines opposite them, their priest held mass and said a prayer for those of them who would die that day in battle, and a big hairy man stood up in back and said, "Father, we want you to pray also for those of our brothers across the way who will be dying today as well."

Which the priest, a Basque himself, did. . . .

That story moved me in much the same way as Pepe Mut's tale of the Italians' rout at Guadalajara which had so elated him and his fellow Nationalist soldiers. The Spanish Civil War had been a ripping, tearing, emotional conflict and its passions were still alive.

The other side's passions had also been still alive in Mexico and New York, when I had lived in those places.

APRIL 23, MADRID: A bit unstrung, have to redo the "Valley" piece [for *Sports Illustrated*] and have just puttered with the
job. Pepe Mut's news about Joe [I have no idea now what this
news was] starting me to brooding again about the Palma expatriate piece, but it is done. Live with your mistakes. Just don't
write again while angry.

Old John: This was excellent advice, and by and large I have
followed it ever since, so maybe that vitriolic little piece of work
was worth the doing. . . . The only other thing I've ever written
that caused me pangs of that sort was a chapter in my 1960 *Goodbye to a River* concerned with the nineteenth-century Truitt-
Mitchell feud in Hood County, Texas, just north of where I now
live. It wasn't an angry chapter, but not much definite was known
about the feud, so that I was fairly free to deal with it as I wished.
I chose to side more or less with the Mitchells, a clan of hardy
frontiersmen (a bend of the Brazos River is still named for them),
rather than with the Truitts, a more civilized and religious but in
my view trickier bunch of townsfolk. At one point there was a
deadly skirmish between the families' males, and afterward the
court testimony of James Truitt, a Methodist preacher, got patriarch Nelson Mitchell, known as Cooney, hanged by the neck
until he was dead, dead, dead, but not before in his last words he
had called upon his absent son Bill, wherever he might be, to
avenge his execution.

Bill had skedaddled after Cooney's arrest, but hadn't forgotten anything. Eleven years later, in 1886, he tracked the Reverend James Truitt to where he now lived in forested East Texas,
entered the house, shot the preacher dead in his rocking chair,
and rode away.

There is quite a bit more to the story, but those were the key
events. When my book was published in 1960, Truitts erupted all
over the place and started writing hostile letters to me and the
publisher. No Mitchells made any sound, for after Cooney's
hanging they had dispersed and Bill Mitchell had lived out his

life in hiding. But the enraged and prolific Truitt faction turned out to include even the mother of a girl I had gone with in high school.

I supposed all that was to be expected and I didn't feel very bad about it, for my account of the feud had made it clear that I was reconstructing events only as I thought they might have been. But then I received a long handwritten letter, mutedly angry but mainly sad, from an eighty-seven-year-old lady in Arizona. As a child, she had been standing beside the chair of her father, the Reverend James Truitt, when Bill Mitchell came into the room and killed him, and she had been living all her life with that scene vivid in her mind.

Is writing an honorable profession? . . .

Whatever Pepe's news about Joe amounted to, other tidings from Palma at about this time were a bit less negative. It seems that drunken Dick Allingham had seduced and impregnated one of his and Carol's young maidservants, an andaluza, and on a moonless night a group of her vengeful male relatives had laid for him in an alley and used fists and clubs to batter him bloody and senseless. . . .

APRIL 26: Finished revision of "A Valley," shortening it by six pages, and think it is o.k. Hope they think so too (∞). I think I may get to work on the drunk dog story next ["The Aztec Dog"]; the novel is getting nowhere.

APRIL 29: Am moving along again. Two or three days' thinking and work on the drunk dog story, which is shaping up, though the old man has become a new character and is taking it over. Anyhow it bucks up my mood a bit. Also am rereading some Ford Madox Ford, and tonight saw the movie of *From Here to Eternity,* which despite being in dubbed Spanish had in it enough of the good things about Americans that I walked out of it somehow proud. A more shapely piece of work than the book was. It also had the useful effect of refocusing me a little—that's where you focus, boy, not here. This sojourn abroad is only to give you perspective on that.

MAY 6: [Much about various pieces of work; I seem to have gotten a little fire under my tail for a change.] Am currently on a reporting piece about the capea/novillada I saw with Alex Brook and Charlotte last Sunday in a pueblo in the mountains, a grimly comic affair. Anyhow I'm getting some work done, but am yearning toward movement on the bigger thing.

My report on these fights in the mountain town's square, blocked off as an arena by carts across the street entrances, was eventually published as "In the Absence of Horses." A couple of young aspirant matadors, one of them American, had bought two three-year-old fighting bulls—novillos—one for each of them to fight, and a cow of fighting blood for the villagers.

But these natives had no intention of being mere spectators at any fight, and the whole thing degenerated into something very much like a capea, one of the violent village bull-baitings, illegal by then for many decades, that had once been a high point of the year in many pueblos. Time after time, drunk peasants with cane stalks and knives and clubs and scythes and hoes distracted the novillos from the capes and muletas of the young toreros, and caused them to botch their swordwork in killing. And when the one-eyed cow that genuinely belonged to the town was released from her box, the bloodiness turned serious. One of the celebrants got gored, and his friends in anger stepped up their sharp-edged attack on the cow.

Alex had seen enough and started for his car, followed by me and reluctantly by Charlotte, who was avid about anything to do with the bulls. But just then the Civil Guardsman who had been sent there to maintain order, an utterly futile assignment, shot the cow dead with his Mauser, terminating the fun.

MAY 11: A Spanish public school teacher takes nine years to obtain his or her bachillerato, three years more to get through the official teachers' school, and one year of training and practice teaching. After all that he receives a job paying four or five hundred pesetas a month [ten or twelve dollars then, at the official exchange rate, or less in terms of the black market], probably under priests' supervision. Pepe Mut's sister and brother-in-law, both of them teachers, getting unconvicted. [I do not recall what this story was, but it involved a difficulty with the clergy.] Some of the finest Spanish jokes are about priests, and Pepe is full of them.

Have been working, I don't know how effectively. But they took the "Valley" piece, which is a kick both psychologically and financially. Think I will go to England in June, do better work, try to corrupt Sam away from his brood into a side trip to France and Spain. Then settle somewhere quiet and simple, maybe in France.

Reading last night the autobiography, "as told to" somebody, of Juan Belmonte, the noted matador from Hemingway's time. Very solid, with the ups and the downs and the self-doubt and the real intelligence and all the Spanish cockiness. A reassuring sort of book like Maugham's *Of Human Bondage,* full of recouped mistakes, the opposite of Puritanism which lets you recoup none at all.

MAY 19: All the stuff I put down in various places above in criticism of current bullfighting is true, and then one windy afternoon with rain threatening, I saw a tiny man called Chicuelo II, taking his Madrid alternativa, work two large and hesitant bulls with such utter valor, such complete and fierily deliberate exposure of himself, and kill them so honestly, that for a moment all the corruption and the brutality and the real boredom of the averagely bad bullfights were beside the point. They said he did not even know a great deal about bulls, nor was he graceful in the manner of the great ones, but those were the last things that mattered.

That was at the annual Madrid fiesta of San Isidro, a high point in the tauromachial year, with a corrida every afternoon for a week. I attended them with Charlotte, who worked at the Madrid office of the U.S. Information Service, later revealed to be CIA. Despite her avidity, or maybe in part because of it, she was great company at bullfights.

MAY 26: Am still trying to get back to work after relaxing last week with the bulls and lousing up my hours. Plus that mess [what mess? I now ask myself], the French girl, this and that and the other and being involved constantly with friends even if it's only for lunch or to go interpret the termination of a contract or the purchase of a dog. Not even further stimulus from Schaffner—another revision to do—has me jumping very hard, though checking this journal's entries from a year ago in Palma shows that I have come a good way. Haven't written a lot but have straightened out, am thinking better, more alive, eye more on the ball. Am looking forward now to a month in Devonshire with Sam—quiet, work, walking, reading. I hope it may help me get perspective on the book. I really need to start it, am getting a little homesick and would very much like to be irrevocably committed on a book, at least, before I go back to the States.

The continuing illusion that geographical change will change other things, specifically me. Sometimes it does. Am a bit tired of here, at least for now. Drinking last night with Jim and Froggy [two of the De Havilland engineers] and the jokes popping rougher and rougher at Angèle the French whore. They are essentially Cockneys with Cockney coarseness and other limitations, though within that context they are solid as rocks and I like them.

Froggy White was the reigning and eldest member of that little group of British engineers, and my favorite among them. In a small hotel in Switzerland that his father had managed, he had grown up speaking not only English but some German and fluent French, which had led to his nickname. And quite soon in his present job, he had attained an adequate command of Spanish as well.

A warm and generous man of about fifty, with graying sandy hair and a little mustache, he was beloved by the Luxor's employees and knew much about their lives and problems. He came to me one day with a proposal. It seemed that one of the waiters in the hotel's small bar and grill, a quick and competent boy named Anastasio, had a chance to be hired at Horcher's, a German restaurant that was one of the two or three fanciest places in Madrid at that time. Even beginning as a busboy there, he would be making at least twice what Gustavo Morales paid him.

The trouble was that he couldn't afford the tailor-made white jackets and dark trousers of a specific design that he would have to own in order to take the job. It was not Anastasio who had told Froggy about this—he was not that sort—but one of the other waiters at the Luxor, from whom Froggy had extracted the details.

Froggy summed up the matter and said, "You're one of those bloody rich Americans, John. Let's go halvers and buy the boy's outfit, and start him on his way."

We did, and shortly thereafter an ecstatic and grateful Anastasio departed the Luxor for a richer realm.

My sparse and spotty income sufficed for fairly easy living in the Madrid of the fifties but did not warrant regular patronage of places like Horcher's or the Jockey Club, where a single meal could run to eight hundred or a thousand pesetas. So I lost sight of Anastasio for two or three months, and indeed just about forgot him. Then a woman friend of mine from Texas stopped off in Madrid and called me. Our friendship dated back to high school days, when she had been close to a girl I was in puppy-love with and I had used her as a confidante. But during and after that time I came to know she was much much smarter than the one I thought I loved. There was never anything amorous between us, but we wrote letters back and forth during college days and the war, and still corresponded from time to time.

And here she was, recently divorced and touring Europe. She had connections at the U.S. embassy and was tied up for most of the few days she would be in Madrid, but she accepted gladly when I asked her to have dinner with me on one of her evenings.

I decided to blow some pesetas on Horcher's. It was a place often sprinkled with visiting celebrities, which we clearly were not, and our reception by the headwaiter was standardly gracious but edged faintly with condescension. He looked over his shoulder and snapped his fingers.

"Anastasio!" he called, and that was who came forward, no longer a busboy but a full-fledged waiter. Only then did I remember that he worked here.

"Bienvenido, Don Juan!" he said, smiling broadly.

The mayordomo regarded his smile with suspicion and told him to show us to a table, pointing toward the far wall of the main room with a particular cock of his eyebrow.

Anastasio and I talked all the way to the table and while he ceremoniously seated us, he filling me in on his career and I him on the latest gossip at the Luxor. Then he pulled himself together, took our order with formality, and disappeared.

My friend Jeanie, who spoke no Spanish, looked at me in puzzlement.

I said merely that this fellow and I had known each other before he started working in the restaurant.

The only celebrities I remember spotting in Horcher's that evening were a movie actress named Linda Christian, once married I believe to Tyrone Power, and the notorious and daring Waffen SS Colonel Otto Skorzeny, who had escaped while awaiting postwar prosecution in Germany and was living quite comfortably in Madrid. But neither their tables nor any others in the place received the kind of attention that our obscurely placed one did. Anastasio saw to it that there were never less than two other waiters in close attendance upon us, and sometimes three, refilling our wineglasses when their level had been lowered by a half-inch or so, and alert to our every whim.

Over dessert and coffee Jeanie, who had enjoyed the meal and our reminiscent conversation but had missed nothing that was going on around us, said, "Now you've got to tell me. Just who the hell *are* you, in this town? How do you get the super treatment?"

So I told her the tale of Anastasio and Froggy White and myself and the waiter uniforms. . . .

MAY 28: Alex Brook's comment on the shabby little men who stand on the long Cortefiel Sastre ribbon-sign during the intervals at the bullfights, keeping it from being blown by the wind: "They also serve who only stand and weight."

A title, from a Leadbelly song: "Who's gonna glove your hand?"

I went up to England shortly after that, catching a ship on the north coast of Spain, and a train from Southampton to Devon where, in a village that seemed to be only lightly brushed by modern times, Sam Hynes and Liz and their two small daughters were living in a thatch-roofed stone cottage, part of which dated to the thirteenth century. Another adult was one too many in that structure, though, so I took a room at the local pub, whose timbers were said to have been shaped from Spanish Armada wreckage. Whether or not this was true, they looked it. The pub's proprietor was a sporting type who kept fighting dogs and a Riley roadster and fed me free Scotch after hours in return for my listening to his recollections of dog battles and car races and cricket matches. Such attention was easy enough, for he was not a bore. His wife, a wan and subdued lady, made some of the best breakfasts I have ever eaten.

I was still fretting myself more or less constantly about not working, or about the quality of what I was doing when I was working, and about the state of the world and so on. I went to London in June and bought a green 250cc BSA motorcycle which was in general a good friend until I sold it much later, before returning to the U.S. However, one of its first actions was quite unfriendly, for immediately after I got back to Ringmore with it, Sam's little one-and-a-half-year-old Joanna managed to pull it over on top of herself where it was parked on its stand, breaking her leg and utterly wrecking his and my plans to go to Pamplona for San Fermín in July. So I stayed on there for a few more weeks, trying to work, taking long talkative walks with Sam up stream valleys to ruined castles or along green clifftops

In motorcycle gear

above the sea. We made friends with the local vicar, a gentle and civilized scion of the Johnnie Walker whisky family, and borrowed field guides to flowers and birds from him. We even identified the scarlet pimpernel. . . .

JUNE 7, RINGMORE, DEVONSHIRE: Immersed in real calm for a change and finding that with a little good company it is possible to enjoy it. Am working. Finished the Whitney bullfight piece (∞) and it is not too bad though it could be better. Now have to redo the "Man Across the Alley" thing and probably can, though I dread the process. This eternal rehashing of things I have done already. A BOOK is what is needed.

This country and what the wars have done to it. The window in tiny Ringmore church with eight or ten names of World War One dead, three of them killed in the one battle of Passchendaele. And the monument on the Hoe in Plymouth, to all those dead at sea, made me feel like weeping. France the same, and Germany and Italy. Played hell with the old world, made it defenseless against things new, killed off the vigorous young ones who might have carried on its ways. Now the new—us, or Russia.

JUNE 13: Finished that "Alley" revision I think competently, am slightly stuck now and don't really want to piddle with any of the other stuff I could piddle with—the shoeshine story, etc. Probably will, though.

What do I really have to say as a writer or a person? This era of suspended breathing and fright in which we live—how can you say anything worth saying about it? You'd be better off ranching or farming or doctoring or in some other of the unquestionable occupations. This mood will pass but it is relevant. I would like so God-damned much to write something worth writing, and if I had the conception I am now competent enough with words to do it. But the conception is hard to come

by. I am tired of working on cheap crap or even on honestly
done vignettes.

Quit whining!

Nearly fifty years later, though, this particular whine looks to
Old John like a near miss in terms of Young John's recognizing
just what his writing problem consisted of. I was trying to blame
my difficulties on the times, I guess, and in general they *were*
poor times, with the accelerating destruction of old human ways
that were dear to me and the glum threat of nuclear warfare
always looming.

But the times weren't really the point. The point, I believe,
was that I was looking for what I called "conception"—subject
matter, really—in a confused way, attempting to write about the
sorts of things that writers I admired had dealt with. I had the
writing disease in excelsis and probably knew by then that it was
a permanent affliction, one I would have to live with. I was getting better and better with words as I kept trying, and I knew
that too. What I didn't see was that I still had to find the subject
matter that was right for me, or had to let it find me. It would
need to define itself, as in fact it ultimately did, for better or
worse, in the provincial Texas environs that had shaped me as a
person.

I don't think this means that the time away from my native
heath and all the missteps and faulty understandings were beside
the point. They were somehow needed to get me wherever it is
that I got to, but I'll come back to that topic further along.

On the motorcycle, I returned to Madrid in July, keeping no
notes during the trip to help me recall it, though I do remember
making a detour to see a sad, half-empty, ancient Castilian stone
village just because of its impossibly beautiful name on the map,
Madrigal de las Altas Torres. Madrid was pretty dead, with most

of the people I knew away, but Pepe Mut had been writing from Palma and it was time for our planned cruise to Ibiza on his sloop *Pegaso*. The record of that voyage runs as follows:

SUNDAY, JULY 18: We spent the afternoon sweating and loading the boat with Pepe Ripoll [a friend of Pepe Mut's who was going along too]. Finally got away at 2035, but in the middle of the bay discovered we had left behind a big tin of olive oil and had to go back for it. Headed for Cabo Figuera, a good night with a light west wind in the beginning, then calming, then a light easterly, also calming. P. Ripoll went to sleep below [he was a friendly little redheaded, freckled guy if not too bright, but his ways were a bit nerve-wracking and sleeping turned out to be his major talent]. At about 0325 at Cala Figuera we caught a good north wind that carried us to the Islas de Malgrat, where we anchored at 0430 and figured to sleep late.

MONDAY, JULY 19: But at 0810 P. Ripoll, having slept long and well, was up and loudly jolly and making coffee for all, so that it was necessary to rise ill-rested and grumpy. They

Dinner with the two Pepes in Cala Fornells

spearfished and got a couple of small specimens, which we fried and ate for breakfast. 1100: Hoisted sail and went to Cala Fornells, where our schedule was slightly messed up by the presence of Sr. Andía and the daughter he was trying to marry to P. Mut, and a Frenchman with whom P. Mut had business.

Much wining and dining, not wise because we were sailing to Ibiza later. At around 2000, tired and groggy, we put to sea on bearing 243°, with a fresh east wind that turned stout as hell once we passed the capes. At around midnight it was necessary to reef the mainsail, take off the large jib, and put on the little one (P. Ripoll sleeping nicely all the time), and the big one eventually blew overboard from atop the cabin, we having forgotten in the stormy uproar to stow it right. Clear moonlight, huge seas, long nightmarish sleepy running before the big wind with the boom far out to starboard, rising up with the waves and sliding down their backs, half-afraid to look back at the next one, scudding through the last of the night-fishing fleet, scared shitless of a broach that would swing us broadside to the combers, watching for the Tagomago lighthouse on Ibiza and finally at around 0300 picking it up.

P. Mut and I were taking turns at the tiller and dozing in the little cabin below and when the steersman was nearly passing out from drowsiness he would slide forward holding the tiller and kick the other fellow awake to take over. P. Ripoll, however, slept quite well the whole while in the other bunk.

At one point when Pepe took the helm from me, he shook his head and rubbed his eyes to awaken more fully. He glanced over his left shoulder at a huge breaking wave and said, "You know, Zhohn, we do it sometimes for the wrong reason. We do it to scare ourselves, a little. There is something wrong with that."

As I grew groggier that night, I had real hallucinations built around that light toward which we steered, the one I remember best being a peasant family sitting around a table with a candle on it (the lighthouse) and having a conversation whose subject I do not recall. The wind and the waves continued beastly strong but we rounded Tagomago in gray dawn light at 0505 and a little later anchored in a mud-bottomed, sheltered cove where we slept until 1300.

Pepe Ripoll woke us once that morning with a mournful wail from the cockpit, over whose gunwale he was sitting with his pants down. "I am stopped up like a bottle!" he cried. "Nothing is passing through!"

"Try some lemon juice and shut up," said my Pepe, and we went back to sleep.

Over a period of about two weeks we circumnavigated the island of Ibiza, not hurrying, putting in at little coves at night—calas, they were called—and buying bread and wine from nearby peasants. Pepe Mut's mother had been born on the island and he spoke its dialect of Catalan, which helped a lot because the country folk knew little Spanish and were even uncomfortable with Mallorquín. Snorkeling, we speared fish and crustaceans and cephalopods, and each day for the big noon meal the Pepes made them into a seafood paella that they called simply "un arroz," a rice. After boiling the morning's catch in water for a time, they would brown the dry rice in olive oil, add hot fish broth and at some point garlic and saffron and salt, then serve the whole lovely mess in bowls. These meals were usually very good, though there were occasional shortfalls, like the day when we got no fish and had to make our rice with limpets picked off of the rocks, extremely tough and not very palatable fare.

WEDNESDAY, JULY 21, CIUDAD IBIZA: Spent the whole day in town. Ran across Anthony Edkins [a wacky, demoralized, educated Britisher I had come to know in Madrid, who made a skimpy living as a guide on tour buses] drinking brandy at a café in midmorning with a friend of his who lives in a whorehouse here.

First fish caught off Ibiza

The day passed nosing around the city, buying supplies, eating cheaply and well. In the evening I had to choose between nosing around some more with the two Pepes and a "funny people party" to which Edkins had invited me, and not feeling up to what E.'s funny people might be like, I chose the former. We went to a nightclub called El Corsario, not much of a place though good and noisy, and we didn't get back to the boat until 0330.

Another thing I remember about Ciudad Ibiza is that we ran out of cigarettes. In cafés the natives rolled their own with local tobacco whose smoke smelled a little like dog turds. When we bought some and tried it, however, it tasted all right to me, though Pepe remained addicted to his Chesterfields and found a black-market source.

There was another resort-city stop at San Antonio Abad on the west coast, where Pepe Mut and I vied for the attention of a slinky, vacationing, bikini-clad German brunette named Hannelöre (I think that umlaut's right), but she didn't give a damn about either of us, just wanted to stay on good enough terms to be taken sailing, which she accomplished. Then there were more days of sailing from cala to lovely cala and spearfishing and swimming and eating our varied paellas, along the steep, rugged, stupendous west side of the island, occasionally getting into tight spots with weather or currents or rocks but always getting out of them thanks to Pepe's intuitive seamanship.

At one point we made an expedition to a very poor farm that should have been depressing but wasn't, and I fictionalized that episode twenty years later as a little chapter in my book *Hard Scrabble,* a part of which I might as well paraphrase here, defictionalized and somewhat shortened.

That day, out of bread and low on wine, we put into a cove with a tiny beach where an old lateen-rigged fishing boat had been pulled up on the sand, a seine spread out beside it to dry. Taking a steep path to the top of the cliffs, Pepe Mut and I came up into a little valley of baked pale earth. Goats were browsing scrub growth on the slopes under the eye of an uncommunicative mongoloid boy, and on the dry valley floor a patch of scrawny American corn clung to life, while farther up among fruit and olive trees there were healthier strips of wheat.

At the head of the valley stood a low house of yellow stone whose short, leathery owner came out to talk with us, accompanied by two little mongoloid girls, while other members of the family, at first, peeked at us from doors and windows. He had bread, yes, plenty of it, the hard, dark, Ibicenco sort that kept forever. He pulled out chairs for himself and us on a gallery looking down the valley to the sea, and served us wine from his own grapes with which we washed down hard salty goat cheese and bitter olives brought by his wife and mother. Pigs and chickens and children and a donkey came to study us as we talked. Knowing me to be no islander, the father spoke in awkward Spanish at times, but always lapsed into dialect when speaking with Pepe Mut, who translated most of it for me.

Three of his eight children, the two little girls and the boy with the goats, were not normal. He spoke of it calmly, a natural misfortune. No, he did not see their life as hard. He had the valley in which grain and fruit and olives could be grown when the rains fell right; his goats, sheep, hogs, and poultry furnished meat; and his oldest son caught plenty of fish from the boat we had seen in the cove. There was more than enough of everything. . . .

He would take no money for the bread, or for the bottles of wine and the fruit that he put into the same sack. At one point I had mentioned seeing ripe roasting ears in the corn patch below, then had had to explain what roasting ears were, which had given both the farmer and Pepe a good laugh, for in Spain corn was strictly animal feed. But as we were leaving he told me to pick as many ears as I wanted, and when we passed the patch I took three.

I could tell that Pepe was much moved by this visit, but he only spoke of it once, as we started down the path to the beach. "Now you have seen my true people, Zhohn," he said. "That man . . . that man is more man than we are. He is . . . *entire*."

I did boil the three small ears of corn that evening, and with olive oil serving as butter mine was quite good. But the two Pepes only nibbled suspiciously at theirs, smirking and shaking their heads.

On our voyage back to Mallorca, in daylight this time, the wind dropped to nothing and we were becalmed for hours out in the middle of blue nowhere, with not a speck of land in sight. The sea was glassy but restless, and as the boat slowly rocked, the mainsail and its boom would slat lazily from side to side within the scope allowed by the tightened mainsheet. Whack, pause. Whack, pause. Whack. . . . The sun bore down and broiled us. I have never been truly seasick, but I came close to it that day.

Blue, deep, open-sea water has always spooked me a little, but it started to look good as we sat there sweating. Finally I stripped down as the two Pepes watched, and dove in. The water was cool and right, and when I surfaced I raised a hand and beckoned. "Come in," I said. "It will wake you up."

Pepe Mut shook his head and grinned his wry grin. "No, Zhohn," he said. "Hay bichos gordos abajo!"

There were fat creatures down below. . . . He would swim out to the middle of Palma Bay and back each morning, but he wanted nothing to do with these unknowable depths so far from any shore. I thought about this for a moment, submerged again, then swam back to the *Pegaso* and pulled myself aboard. I was not so big on fat sea creatures myself. . . .

A strong southeast wind did finally blow in, and we hit Mallorca at Andraitx where the Germans had had a submarine base in World War Two. From there we sailed around Cabo Figuera into Palma Bay and made it to the Club Náutico at last, with a curiously empty but contented feeling of having "done it." It really was quite a voyage in a twenty-three-foot wooden boat with no auxiliary power.

In a funny way, being mutually and irritably amused by P. Ripoll's constant sleeping in times of crisis or hard work, his ill-timed heartiness, and his eternal complaints about constipation, had drawn P. Mut and me closer together. The contretemps with the umlauted German girl had done that too, because we both knew how to laugh at things and at each other. He was a hell of a man and a hell of a friend, and it tore me when he died of lung cancer (Chesterfield brand, I suppose) three or four years after I came back to the States. We had corresponded fairly often, but then there was a gap, and finally a letter came from his brother Roberto telling what had happened.

Back in Madrid the night clerk at the Luxor, a stubborn, humorous young rustic Castilian named Paco Hernández, talked me

The Pegaso

into taking him on my motorbike to his home pueblo of Mombeltrán in the Gredos mountains, where the annual harvest festival was about to begin. It was a stirring and rather wild affair
that lasted for a week. The village sprawled beneath the ramparts of a ruined castle, and under great black poplars by its clear
river young people danced all night long to pagan music from
gaitilla pipes, though some couples wandered off into the woods
to assess each others' charms. During the day there was eating,
with food laid out wherever you went, and never-ending visits to
people's individual cool wine caves in the mountainside, where
their year's fermentation was stashed in enormous earthen

tinajas—amphorae in shape, but holding at least eighty or a hundred gallons each. After you had drunk you praised the wine even when it was bad, then smashed your clay cup on the floor.

I stayed gratis at the little inn run by Paco's family—his father had been mayor there during the Republic—and in the evenings sat on the castle ramparts with a fireworks man named Parriga, helping him ignite his chain explosions and flares and pinwheels and rockets to applause from down below. Everywhere I went I was greeted as Paco's friend. They had never seen an American before.

Like the hardy, generous Ibizan farmer in his little valley, these folk lived chiefly on what they raised in the way of grapes, grain, olives, vegetables, and small livestock, and they lived pretty well. Up the mountain a few miles, though, was another village whose soil was mainly rocks, and I was told that the people there had to get through the winters on chestnut gruel and a little goat meat.

AUG. 21, MADRID: A rather large and relieving thought while lying in bed this morning, provoked in part by Abe Rothberg's letter the other day about his recent visit with Bryan. He says that he finally understands what I went through with her. I have felt rightly guilty about all that, and about leaving her and so on. Oh God, have I ever! But now it comes to me also that there are things for me to forgive her for. The black self-pitying melancholy that would hit her when I was feeling "up" (really, I came to believe, *because* I was feeling up), and I would have to go down into the depths with her and expend myself in bringing her back. Obviously it was beyond her control and I do forgive her, but this new awareness, that all that was not one-sided, is a healthy one.

Reading: George Sessions Perry, *Hold Autumn in Your Hand*. It is a good piece of work, and causes me no envy because Texas is not my territory any more.

[Old John: This was a *very* major misapprehension, as things turned out, for in the long run Texas was the main territory I did have.]

The book has a few small patches of slickness but not many, and it catches the good-humored charm and the solidity of the best country Texas people. Tom Lea, *The Brave Bulls*. Very solid though sometimes awkward, but not in the Cuenca Plaza climax which is powerful. You can tell he is a painter, and his writing is flavored like his painting—heroic. Slocum, *Sailing Alone Around the World*. It affects me like Anson's *Voyages*— they made them tough back then, tough and strong and monolithic. Lowry, *The Wolf That Fed Us* (stories). A lot of sharp perception, some really lovely writing, and one long whine of pity for himself and the world. Shelby Foote, *Follow Me Down*. Faulkner simplified and brought up to date but not as good, though pretty good at that. A faulty technique—first-person multifaceted a little like *As I Lay Dying* and with the same trouble that book has, i.e., raising the obtrusive question of how these simple people can express themselves so eloquently.

The resentful dislike which many Americans abroad feel toward other Americans for being there too, and which at bottom is probably a nervousness about *being* American.

A small restaurant in a side street near the Ministry of the Army, with marble-topped tables and solid pueblo-style food— white beans with sausage, suckling lamb chops, kidneys in sherry, good Valdepeñas vino corriente. A lot of men ate there alone; the place always had reasonable business but never a crowd. Some of the people were vaguely literary, and from time to time there were young bullfighters who spoke loudly to one another to cover up the fact that they couldn't afford fancier places. Before the Civil War García Lorca had come there often and the present proprietress, a sweet-faced woman who had been very young then and whose parents had run the place, remembered him reciting his poems to friends and that he always ate raw garlic with whatever he ordered. The floor was tiled and most of us who ate there knew one another's faces without knowing names to go with them. We would nod and say "Aproveche!" the bon appétit of Spain. The little lamb chops fried in olive oil were very very good, and when you had finished eating, if you were alone and had nowhere else you wanted to go, you could sit there until midnight smoking, drinking the sweetish wine or coffee, and reading a book or writing letters.

That season in Madrid I was alone a great deal, mainly by choice. It was one of the better cities I had known to be alone in, not so big that loneliness surrounded you and piled up as it could in New York, nor so active and vibrating that the mere fact of being by yourself amid so much movement and companionship cut you, as in Paris, like a knife.

SEPT. 3: Finding Jim Phillips in the Luxor bar at breakfast yesterday morning, one of those coincidences that can't be a coincidence, and talking all afternoon during lunch and a Turkish bath and drinks and on through a bottle of Carlos I coñac, about writing and Fort Worth and being American and everything. Damned nice to run into someone from my own background who also cares about writing.

Recognizing him across the room that morning, I went over to his table and said, "You've got to be Jim Phillips."

He started and sloshed his coffee. "And just who the hell are you?" he demanded.

I told him and he nodded, appeased. "Olcott told me to look you up over here," he said. "But we've never crossed paths till now."

Olcott was his younger brother, a lawyer in Fort Worth and a good friend of mine to this day, though Jim had been enough older when I was growing up that I had barely known him. In the late 1930s he had published an angry-young-man's novel ripping the curtains aside from the foibles and amorous intrigues of the city's country-club set. It was well written and received much scandalized or titillated attention in Fort Worth, though I don't think a great deal elsewhere. He had married one of the prettiest girls in town, a doctor's daughter, and had moved to New York to take over the literary world but somehow, like multitudes of us others, had failed to achieve that goal.

Over the years he had published things in the big slick magazines of the day, such as *Collier's,* and was still doing so but less often. I believe that by the time I saw him in Madrid (it may have been somewhat later) he had come down to turning out paperback spy thrillers one after another, rather shoddy ones but they sold enough to keep him living well.

Where he was living well just then was on Tenerife in the Canaries, and the glowing terms in which he spoke of it as a place to work started me thinking about going there to try it for myself. At the moment he was on his way to Scandinavia to marry a Swedish baroness with whom he had been living on Tenerife and who had told him, in effect, "Marry me or leave me alone." He was full of doubts about the matter, having had mainly trouble with women—and with a lot of other people too, for in many ways Jim *was* trouble, as I well knew from hearing stories about him from Olcott.

But I was glad to see him and we talked our heads off for three or four days and rode my motorbike down to Aranjuez to see a bullfight. After he headed on north toward matrimony I was stirred up enough by all our talk that I started scribbling lengthy notes and passages for the novel I was planning to write.

SEPT. 8: A Spanish movie, *La Patrulla,* about a group of friends from the Legión Azul in the years since the Eastern Front. Essentially propagandistic, in terms of the need to fight Reds wherever they are. Also spoiled by sentimentality, though it does capture some good things like the compañerismo of war. Jesus, what books and movies they *could* make of all that has happened here in twenty years, if there was anyone with the impartiality or just the bigness to do it right. But there probably isn't—we Americans ourselves have not averaged one really good book per war throughout our history.

Old John: Some Spanish writers I read later did write decently about that era. Particularly memorable were books by José María Gironella and Arturo Barea. Young John was quite a generalizer. . . .

The Blue Legion, a volunteer Falangist force, has been mentioned before in these pages. One of Franco's main contributions to the German war effort, it was miserably clobbered by the Russians.

SEPT. 11: The Spanish stare on trains and in cafés—when I hit it again after long absence it bothers me again, and I fall back on an old countermeasure. Sitting down, I start unobtrusively to study the starer's feet and ankles, and then when, not being able to help it, he glances down and then up again, I smile and angrily he looks away. It works every time, but after a while I don't need it. I just ignore the stare, as I always have in the past.

SEPT. 29: On the motorbike through green Aranjuez and up the dry rocky valleyside to Ocaña, then forking left into the wide dry rich plains of La Mancha. It is the Quixote country— Quintana de la Orden and squat windmills and anciently fortified farms, and not far south of the main road are Toboso where Dulcinea dwelt, and Tomelloso where in jail for debt Cervantes may or may not have begun to write the book; some sources put that jail in Sevilla. Sheep and vineyards and old stone threshing floors on which wheat is still winnowed in the eternal breeze by leather-faced men with wooden pitchforks, and once when a Spanish friend of mine asked to have his car washed in a village there, they did it with wine because there was more of that than of water.

The motorbike was a joy for trips and explorations. Back then, there were few cars on Spanish roads and hence few traffic dangers. As you cruised along at forty or fifty miles an hour, you were at one with all of the rolling countryside's smells and sights and with its very feel, hitting layers of settled cool air as you dropped down into the valleys, then rising again into the dry Castilian heat. Mechanically the little machine was just about perfect; the only time I had trouble with it was because I wasn't yet fully tuned in to the quirks of motorcycles. This happened in the garage where I kept it in the city. When I mounted and kicked the starting lever, the engine backfired, the carburetor burst into flames, and before an attendant and I finally smothered the fire, the bike's wiring had been badly burned and had to be replaced.

Afterward Tavo Morales told me (all Spaniards who could afford them had gone through a motorbike phase) that what I should have done was to keep kicking until it started, which would have sucked the flames into the motor and put them out. . . .

SEPT. 30: Nothing constructive of late except a "Javanese" exotic nightclub dancer who bills herself as Princess Ming Chu and is quite generous with her charms. . . . From her looks (good) and the Spanish she speaks, I would guess her to be half-Chinese and the other half Latin American of some sort.

OCT. 15: Working at present on "Friends of the EE. UU.," which will turn out one way or another but is overloaded right now.

I have searched my records for mention of this piece of writing and its fate, but there is none, so I assume it remained unpublished. I don't even remember its subject, or whether it was an essay, a short story, or an article intended for a magazine.

"EE. UU." is the Spanish abbreviation of "Estados Unidos," meaning the good old U.S.A.

OCT. 18: Pepe Mut is in town and we have resumed the old sauntering after-supper chats. When he gets absorbed in making a point he takes your elbow and pumps it up and down. I am supposed to go up to Ávila to see Tony but haven't gotten around to it. The bluff, wholly American artist Harry Jackson and with him much drinking of wine and much exchange of philosophy esthetic and otherwise, a hell of a fellow. Sage and Martha Schaff who don't like me for the Palma article—his mother lives there and has taken the piece very hard. Joining the British-American Club—why?

The main answer to that, I think, is that I was interested in a chastely inaccessible but charming English girl named Olga, who worked at the British embassy and took part in amateur Shakespeare productions at the B-A Club. I told her once that I wouldn't mind acting in one of the plays myself, and she couldn't control her mirth. "Just fancy!" she said. "An American speaking Shakespeare's lines! And with a Texan accent, at that!"

She knew how to keep you in your place, Olga, and she was rather unflappable. Once when I took her to Valladolid for a bullfight, she riding pillion on the motorbike, the town's streets had been watered against dust and, going slow, I hit a wet tram track diagonally, flipping the machine onto its side and skidding us along the cobblestones. It ruined the elbow of my blazer (I still have that garment, its damage rewoven by Spanish nuns) and one of Olga's stockings, with some abrasion to her leg. But when I got the bike upright again she said, "Let's go. We'll be late."

OCT. 20: Reading Madariaga's *España,* maybe the best thing I've gotten hold of on the general subject. A couple of bad bull-fights and missing the ones up in Zaragoza, and so on, and it all sounds like more than it is. Am at least working a little, and relevantly, because this story is parallel to the book.

One of the worst things that's happened in the past few years was the taking over of that section of South Carolina by the Atomic Energy Commission, almost as bad as the fact that those happy lost Stone Age tribesmen in New Guinea were "found" and are going to be civilized.

OCT. 26: Hunting rabbits with Tavo Morales Sunday in the open country north of here, where he has landowning friends. Eating in Colmenar, and the tough, weathered old man who runs the bull ranch there—except for the language he speaks he could have come straight out of West Texas.

The international-set types who can make one form or another of nothing seem extremely important, until you look at it closely.

On that rabbit hunt with Tavo Morales we separated for a while to cover more ground, and at one point I came upon a scene that I have written about elsewhere, in a passage that may be worth repeating here:

A soft-spoken decent man in beret and smock encountered one day as I walked down a swale in the rolling untimbered foothills of the Guadarrama. . . . He was lying at ease on the slope, a short distance away from a collection of small birds that were warbling and cheeping in wicker cages or from twigs to which they were leg-tethered. On the grass he had spread fine-meshed nets to be sprung when enough wild ones had gathered to these decoys. He got very little recompense for his catch, he said, but it was what he did, his living and his father's before him. Species didn't matter much—thrushes, finches, larks, whatever came—because the wineshops in Madrid that bought them from him would pluck them anonymous and gut them and fry them crisp in oil. I had seen them in such places in platters on the bar, and the accepted etiquette seemed to be to bite the head off first and crunch it with relish before devouring the remainder, bones and all.

Thus not a great deal had changed, though I was getting a little work done and was still thinking about the novel and writing down those thoughts. Harry Jackson, the artist mentioned above, became a close friend eventually. We cottoned to each other partly because we were both Westerners (he had run away from home in Chicago as a kid and had grown up mainly on a Wyoming ranch, cowboying) and partly because we had both been combat Marines in the war, but mainly because we liked to argue and talk about art and writing and a number of other shared interests. In New York he had been in on the start of Abstract Expressionism before veering away from it ("I always get off the train just before it reaches the station," was his comment on this), was a good friend of Jackson Pollock's, and had been married to the painter Grace Hartigan, the first of his four or five wives. At the time I met him in Madrid—through Tony Stubbing, to whom he had been sent by someone—he was visiting the great museums of Europe, sketching and thinking and making notes.

Tony was in the saintly old mountain stronghold of Ávila in nominal charge of a grim mansion belonging to the colorful and slightly mad Duchess of Valencia, who was off somewhere with her current lover, an exiled Albanian who claimed to be a count, though Tony said he was sure the title was bogus. One of the intriguing things about Tony was the connections he could turn up with and never bothered to explain. This one I am sure was based somehow on family, for the upper layers of English and

Spanish society had always had relationships and some intermarrying over the years, and Tony's mother was the daughter and sister of British dukes. At any rate he did have the connection, and the mad Duchess Luisa trusted him enough to put him in temporary command of her house and blooded horses and servants—all but one, an indomitable, square-built, fierce woman cook whose normal voice was a hoarse angry shout. Tony referred to her as "Old Trumpet-Twat," but he feared her as did everyone else in that gloomy gray palace built against the gloomy gray northern wall of that gloomy gray city, where its best-known native, Saint Teresa, was often almost visible.

She was definitely visible in a tale told me by an American from Iowa whom I knew slightly in Madrid. He had married a Spanish nobleman's daughter and had converted to the Church, used a Purdey badly at pigeon shoots, and was in many ways more self-consciously noble than any of the nobility I had seen or met, which was very few. The Iowan once told me, when I mentioned Ávila, how Santa Teresa had saved the city during the Civil War, which he called, in good rightist style, El Movimiento, The Movement.

It was said that one evening when all of the Nationalist soldiers garrisoned there were away fighting elsewhere, an army of Reds had showed up outside the city walls.

"Whose army?" I asked, but he said he didn't know; what did it matter?

And the Reds had had the intention of sacking the city the following morning. But during the night a female figure in luminous robes had wandered around inside their camp and scared them and set them to squabbling among themselves, and in the morning they had packed up and gone away. . . .

When I expressed mild disbelief he said, "Yes, but isn't it a pretty story?"

Tony's Duchess was the one who used to demonstrate from a balcony in Madrid when Franco rode by in parades, not from

Republican sympathies but because she wanted the monarchy restored. I never met her, but I could feel her sense of momentous personal destiny, in mottoes on the walls of that house and in other evidence all around.

OCT. 29, ÁVILA: An inscribed tile, hung on a wall alongside spurs and knives:

NO PUEDO TENER MIEDO
NO PUEDO ENAMORARME
NO PUEDO ESTAR ENFERMA

LUISA VALENCIA

(I MUST NOT BE AFRAID. I MUST NOT FALL IN LOVE. I MUST NOT BE ILL.)

Another elsewhere, with the same signature:

MI CUERPO NO SABE DONDE
LE LLEVA LA VOLUNTAD

(MY BODY DOES NOT KNOW WHERE MY WILL CARRIES IT.)

This is not 1954 or anything within four centuries of it. Nor is it particularly sane, and neither is the big half-furnished (though jammed in spots), half-lived-in house with old Spanish masters on the walls, and copies of old masters, and signed lithograph portraits of royalty from 1860 or so. Everywhere there are pottery and junk and coats of arms. Of living residents, Tony says that by his count there are thirteen servants including the stable hands, seventeen dogs, innumerable cats, two parrots, seven canaries, five horses needing daily exercise, a donkey, a goat, and a caged eagle.

At intervals all day, every day, the eagle screams "Whaik! Whaik! Whaik!" in protest against his incarceration. He is fed on chopped lung, and just about everything else except the horses eats garbanzo peas. . . .

Across the stable's stone wall is a large black-painted scrawl: VIVA D. JUAN III. The butler is an elegant liveried pansy, scared to death of Old Trumpet-Twat, who has taught one of the parrots to screech, "Ma-ric-a! Maricón!" whenever he comes in sight. On the mantel of the fireplace in the new library under construction upstairs, the Albanian boyfriend's coat of arms is to be carved alongside the duchess's, and Tony, who is supposed to be working on their portraits, is painting contorted nudes instead. No, not sane, but much of it is charming—like, T. says, the crazy, beautiful, forceful woman it reflects.

And Tony himself—I'd like to understand him better. Undoubted brains and talent, full of rather shocking cynical attitudes and utterances born of rebellion. The enormous dispersal of his energy in doing so God-damned many things, tiring of one and whipping on to another. Much of it is a cover-up. Telling me to marry a Spanish girl for contentment and service, then Rosemary lighting into him furiously, a true termagant, the other day when we came home late from wherever we had been dawdling and talking.

OCT. 31, MADRID: [Evidently I was doing a bit of traveling back and forth between Ávila and the capital in here.] A dance at the British-American Club, mainly dull. But there was a lot of talk, the best of it with the vigorous, alive Basque querida of an English bore. How much woman they can be at their best. I could marry one if I found the right one and thought I could manage her. Olga was burned at me for spending so much time with the Basque mistress, though the Englishman was glassy-eyed from drink and didn't care.

Horses the other day with Tony, who with one of the grooms exercises them daily. He tricked me onto a big unruly black stallion to see if I could manage him, and I more or less did. I have ridden little since Mexico in '46 and was reluctant, maybe afraid, but I had forgotten how fine it is. A big, head-throwing, hardmouthed son of a bitch, all that power under you, your legs lacking grip from want of that kind of use, but your hands still better than the grooms'.

After one wild downhill dash during which I had had to just let the headstrong studhorse have his way, hoping he wouldn't collide with one of the numerous boulders, Tony on a quiet bay mare was waiting for me at the bottom, laughing as I pulled the big beast to a stop.

"He'd have had you off if you'd gone on a bit farther," he said.

Exhilarated, I said, "The hell he would have!" I knew that quite possibly Tony was right, but just then I didn't give a damn.

Much journalistic grousing here about my work habits and my general aimlessness. These many years later, I can see that if I had been truly aimless—without the writing impulse—I'd probably have been much happier. But I wouldn't have been over there in Spain, either.

NOV. 3, MADRID: Finished "EE. UU." and with a great deal of revision it might come out to be something. Might not, too. I wish I could hit a rule about the stories that turn out and those that don't, so as to quit wasting time and wordage on the failures.

Saw *Don Juan Tenorio* last night, nice with powerful scenes and language despite some shaky acting. The actor playing Don Juan himself had a very bad cold, which at times led to unintended humorous effects, but the old Castilian really rings.

NOV. 5, ÁVILA: A fine trip up yesterday, with Tony on the back of the bike, through San Martín and all the other lovely grim stone villages. Cranes passing over in migration to Africa,

swarms of partridges on the estate where Franco hunts, Castilla
spreading out wide around us, all the peasants staring at
bearded Tony as we passed. He is boyish and good company
when he is enjoying himself. There is also much warmth and
affection underneath his excessive rationality, the latter being I
think the result of many things, among them a rebellion against
family, being bounced by a beloved fiancée at eighteen, then
having another die after the war, and now all this damned
struggling poverty.

Tony's rebellion against his family remained an enigma to
me. I think it was something he needed to do for reasons unre-
lated to rational motive. He told me that his people had written
him off because he had "married a black woman," but once
when I visited his parents in London at his behest, to pick up
some of his possessions, his mother was a gracious, intelligent,
total lady who invited me to a superb supper in their home and
wanted to know all about Rosemary, whom she evidently liked
very much. Her husband was a very reticent retired-colonel
type, clearly fascinated by the maverick son he had sired and
reluctantly proud of him, and many years later Tony told me, on
that visit he paid to us in Texas, that his father had finally shot
himself.

NOV. 6: "EE. UU." will be all right in time. I will go to the
Canaries and will write some kind of a book. Also will live to
be a hundred, very wealthy and wise and famous. . . .
    It has rained all day long here, sad and cold. Ávila seems to
affect me badly, and I think I'll leave about Sunday. Am not
working, though Tony is.
    This God-damned Trumpet-Twat woman here, with the
power and the brassy arriero's voice. Everybody including Tony
is scared of her. It is funny how patterns repeat themselves in
rich people's confidential servants—I have known Negroes

working for Texas oilmen who were much like this peasant bitch. Duchess Luisa is shaping up in my mind as nuttier and nuttier. The little contractor the other night being doubtful to Tony about the orders the "count" had left concerning details of construction in the library, mainly involving his own coat of arms in the carved-stone mantelpiece. "You know how she is," he said, meaning that the Albanian is only one more in a series of five or six dismissed lovers.

An idea born of watching Tony's precipitate work methods: I could make a list of eight or ten stories from the past two years' experience, slap them out one a day, getting them done any old way, then look to see if any is worth a damn. Some possibles: Mrs. Pemberton's illness; Margarita and the estra-perlista; the Ibiza trip including Edkins, the German girl, etc.; Swede's death; the gossip on 15th Street; the trip to La Fossa; a hunting tale maybe mixed with the bulls and roast lamb; Mombeltrán, maybe focusing on Parriga and me and the fireworks on the castle ramparts.

NOV. 7: Getting furious at Tony last night in a more or less political argument with a few drinks taken, slamming off to bed, and then in the anger understanding much more about him than I ever have before. He has carried to an extreme the tendency most of us have to alter facts when fitting them into views we find comforting or useful. He has bound these views in iron and has assembled all sorts of half-facts, misinformation, and bald-faced absurdities to support them. He is Madariaga's Englishman forging a philosophical framework for action, and it seems to serve him very well even though it limits his good mind. And it is baffling as hell if you're damned fool enough or drunk enough to argue against it, as people have noted of the English for a long long time. Some tenets that T. will hold to at least in argument: Any woman will do for any man, the rationale of an uncomfortable marriage; in art, what he does is right and all the rest is trash; all Americans are materialistic and stand for nothing at all; the British Empire was "accidental," rather than exploitative; etc., etc. We covered a range of subjects and he had dubious statistics for his views— the prevalence of infidelity in American women and of frigidity in Spanish women, whether or not Spanish explorers were subsidized by the government, the ethics of the Eisenhower-Franco air base agreement . . .

He was, however, a decent guy who liked me and I liked him, and not much of the rancor of the evening carried over into morning. "I hope you weren't really browned last night," he said in greeting.

"I guess I was. I must have been."

"I just like to stir things up, drinking . . . Don't care bloody all about politics and all that."

We were in the large upstairs room he used as a studio, and suddenly he stalked to a corner to dig out from behind splotched canvases a peeled, rather crooked tree branch with a salmon gaff lashed to one branch of a fork at the top and a sharp-pointed ferrule at the tip with which he gouged at the floor.

"Wonderful stick," he said. "Made it myself."

"You'd never know it," I said.

"Walking stick." He demonstrated. "Wading staff." He leaned against it as though resisting the surge of a great river. "Gaff." He hooked viciously at the air. "And when you don't need it you can just stick it in the ground, and it'll be there when you come back."

This bit of clowning served to clear the air, and I laughed. In spite of his offish and unpredictable ways, there was some real friendship between us.

NOV. 8: It was rather good for me really, getting into a tough angry argument; it made me define the way I feel about a number of things that America means to me. Mainly what T. was holding to was a standard pettily jealous European view of prosperous America, in part sincere but in larger part just to piss me off. It flavors his attitude toward Alex Brook too, of whom he is similarly jealous. I wish I were better able to judge painting—I tend to think Tony is quite good, though the sketches he made of me are not stupendous and his other portraits seem in some ways wooden. I have a strong feeling that he needs to concentrate on detail and dwell more on it, but on the other hand devotion to such detail is a vice in my own work and slows me down badly.

In retrospect, Old John can see that one of Tony's chief skills was in getting Young John's goat, which he could do more effectively than almost anyone I remember. Usually, I am sure, Tony knew quite well when he was being outrageous. In part this was an aspect of his need to keep the rest of the world including me at arm's length, and I don't know why I didn't recognize it as such, for at that time I had something of the same need myself.

NOV. 9: He can be damned funny, Tony. The other day we ate in a little restaurant here in Ávila and the rightist waiter, finding out T. was English (how could he miss it?), treated us to a diatribe about British perfidy in holding on to Gibraltar. Later in the afternoon when we passed that place again, Tony went to the door and crooked a finger at the waiter, saying, "Pssst!" The waiter came over and Tony leaned toward him conspiratorially and whispered loudly in Spanish, "I come to sell you . . . Hee-bral-tar!"

A somehow heartening sign from another era on a wall in Ávila, painted out long ago and now showing through again:

MUERAN LOS GOBIERNOS TRAIDORES AL
   TRABAJADOR.
VIVA EL 1° DE MAYO Y LA ALIANZA OBRERA
   Y CAMPESINA.

It is only heartening because Franco is now in charge, but it shows that there were once other views, doctrinaire though they may have been.

Tavo Morales and his comfortable mistress and his beloved little illegitimate son whom he took me to see the other night, as a major confidence. The fear of his old mother that keeps him from marrying her. He is bound up so tightly in convention that he seems stiff much of the time around people. Most of his employees at the hotel don't like "Don Gustavo" and my friendship with him creates a bit of comical byplay between me and them, since they do like me and most feel Spanishly free to air their views. (María the wizened Castilian chambermaid, venomously: "And how is your friend *Tavo?*")

NOV. 12, MADRID: A movie, *The Caine Mutiny,* dubbed into Spanish. The good things about America and Americans and some of the bad as well. As for all the carping, petty, anti-American crap like Tony's, it doesn't really matter. Some of it is valid and you need to bear that in mind. But you are a part of the American whole, bad and good, and if you try to be anything else wholly, you are nothing.

Have been working today on the Stubbing fast-run principle, and dashed off a number of pages to complete the La Fossa story, probably very badly. Let it rest a while and see. [Since there is no later mention of this masterpiece in the journal, I assume that it turned out awful.]

A random thought: Spain is much like the American South in some ways, the old values still holding out, producing similar good types and similar bad ones. They won one fight against the new values, but even then they had already lost the big fight, simply by being fated to exist in a changing world.

NOV. 15: You seem to have a penchant for bad evenings at about this time of year, just before leaving places. At Joe's last year with Cochrane running amok and whacking everybody, and this past Saturday at the Little Theater group's party, unable to jell with anybody and finally insulting some of them and angering Olga, a horrid evening and my own moody fault, for most of those are worthwhile folks.

Soon thereafter, still in a disgruntled mood, I headed south on the motorbike, a lone and lonely and uncomfortable trip. I cruised the first day through bitter Castilian cold to Manzanares and a rather unpleasant inn, where a Basque officer regaled me at the bar with Spanish clichés about Reds and how Frenchwomen couldn't resist Spanish men and other such pleasant subjects. On the morrow I plugged along still cold through Valdepeñas and over a spur of the Sierra Morena into rich red-and-green Andalucía, stopping for the night in Carmona, then finally, cold all the way, made a run past aristocrats' country mansions, stone-fenced fighting-bull pastures, and sherry bodegas, ending finally at the old port of Cádiz where the treasure fleet used to bring gold and silver from the Americas. There, two days later, I loaded myself and my bike onto a ship bound for the Canaries.

NOV. 23, ABOARD THE *VILLA DE MADRID*: Caught a cold on that frigid motorbike ride to Cádiz, but it's better now. Have met a couple of good canarios aboard, doctors, and am looking forward to the islands. They sound all right, in terms of not only climate but people, who are [Young John seems to have started generalizing very early on this trip] less formal than Spaniards, sort of South American. So perhaps if the foreigners there turn out badly, it will be possible to live with the natives. We'll see.

High dark red-edged stormclouds over Africa at dawn. The magic feeling—you get it more seldom nowadays, but you ought to be glad you can still get it at all.

NOV. 24, STILL ABOARD AT THE WHARF IN LAS PAL-MAS: Don't get all heated up about where you live down here, as you did in Mallorca. If this Puerto de la Cruz where Jim Phillips is living on Tenerife turns out badly, just get the hell out without fanfare. The motorbike gives you mobility and you can make the best of whatever place.

The younger doctor is a nice kid, fresh and idealistic and intelligent. Funny how you can get philosophical on ships—or traveling in general—exposing inner thoughts to someone you didn't know at all a couple of days before. But it is a little like a war, where you get to know people faster, and often you're not going to see them again.

Before going ashore at Las Palmas on Gran Canaria, his home island, the young doctor said while shaking my hand, "You are not as Americans are supposed to be."

"There are plenty more like me, more or less."

"Menos mal," he said. Less bad. "America may be our future."

SIX

Tenerife and Going Home

(1954–1955)

ROM LAS PALMAS we sailed to the harbor of Santa Cruz de Tenerife, where in 1797 Horatio Nelson had lost his right arm during an ill-advised assault on the Spanish defenders. I loaded my suitcase, typewriter, and self onto the motorbike and scooted across the green and rolling divide to Puerto de la Cruz on the island's northwestern shore, where Jim Phillips was living with his willowy ash-blonde baroness Lill, her little girl, and the child's Swedish nurse. I took a room nearby, and from the first saw much of them, having supper there many evenings and staying to drink the Grand Macnish with Jim, straight-malt stuff and cheap in that duty-free place. Sometimes at midnight we would sip good French champagne in their wide-windowed house on a cliff above the pounding Atlantic, a dramatically upper-class setting for Jim's fundamentally dramatic soul.

This rather constant association was not exactly a matter of choice on my part, but had much to do with the fact that after about a month of marriage (and a few months of living together as free agents before that) they were developing tensions, and having me around, almost underfoot in truth, was a way to avoid facing these. Sadly, the whole atmosphere reminded me of the way things had developed between Bryan and me five or six years before, with the differences that this was a second go-around for both of them, the marriage was barely started, and alcohol had not been a factor in my own conjugal crash. Lill, very much a woman as Bryan was, was similarly not content with a woman's lot as generally defined, and would often go melancholy when we two males were talking about books and writing. She was a baroness only through her first marriage (wherefore I judge she was no longer a baroness at all, though in a similar situation the Danish Baroness Blixen, a.k.a. Isak Dinesen, retained the title to the end—without, however, remarrying) and she had had minor parts in two or three Swedish films.

Jim and I ruminated a lot about our Fort Worth background, mainly because he seemed to want to. I had executed a mild withdrawal from that background, which was pretty much standard hinterland American, by choosing a different path in life from the paths of my high school friends. But Jim had rebelled more dramatically, as I've noted, by writing an enraged novel that in its turn had enraged the city's Establishment leaders and most of their kin. Both of us had grown up more or less on the edge of its social world, coming from "nice" families that didn't have much money, but that fact had graveled him far more harshly than it had me, and it still did.

Once there in Puerto, late on a Scotch-drinking night, he said, "If I could have my dearest wish fulfilled, do you know what I would do?"

I didn't.

"I would buy a pretty little atom bomb, and at cocktail hour one afternoon I would drop it down the chimney of the Men's Bar at River Crest Country Club."

As veterans will, we talked a little too about our war, ten years behind us now, during which he had been with the outfit that flew transport planes across the Hump from Assam to Kunming, carrying supplies to bolster Chiang Kai-shek's forces in their own fight with the Japanese.

Lill's older sister Caisa was also in Puerto, married to a man named Norman something-or-the-other, a rich (or what passed for it then and there) and alcoholically paranoid American with an intensely protective attitude toward her daughters from another marriage, and a related hostility toward young Spaniards. The rest of the fairly small foreign colony there, as I remember them, were predominantly Scandinavian and British, and their partying was much less demoralized than what I had seen in Mallorca. There was also some association with upper-class Spaniards from the nearby lush Valley of Orotava where they owned banana plantations, and with a little group of polyglot papal nobility of several nationalities, who also had plantations and spent their summers in attendance on the pope at Castel Gandolfo.

The only one of these latter whom I got to know particularly was a young German count from the Sudetenland, who at the age of fifteen, in the desperate last days of the European war, had been yanked out of military school, commissioned as an officer, and put in charge of a rear guard of reluctant old men. He liked Americans because once when he had blundered with his decrepit troops straight into the line of fire of an American machine gun emplaced in a building's window, the sergeant in charge had seen what a pathetic crew they were and had not fired but had shouted angrily with a wave of his arm, "Get the hell out of here!" which indeed they had done.

Another of these gentry was a strikingly handsome dark-haired young woman from Hamburg, married to a titled Italian. Unlike my friendly count, she abominated Americans and lashed into any unfortunate member of that nationality, including me, who ventured to open his mouth in her presence. This hatred stemmed from the enormously destructive bombing of her home city by our planes during the war, whose details she would recount with vituperative thoroughness, nor could you hint at similar sins on the part of the Luftwaffe without bringing on a second eruption.

Puerto de la Cruz was a lovely place, with its cliffs, its broad rolling ocean, and a superb beach that drew a continual but not overwhelming flow of prosperous European tourists. It had fancy shops, too, including one operated by a Swedish modiste, who brought six or eight comely models with her each winter to show off her creations and, incidentally, to foment excitement and amorous competition among the young scions of the Orotava rich. This lady took an instant dislike to me for no reason I could discern, something that has happened a couple of other times in my life, always inexplicably. Maybe she too hated Americans. She even spread some false tales about my activities—lewd advances toward one of her models, for instance—which were reported to me by another Puerto resident, a friendly Scotswoman named Mollie, who viewed the tales with amusement. She said, "That's just the way that one is. I think she's partly Laplander witch."

The Laplander witch aside, I liked Puerto and the people there. But I had work on my mind, specifically the novel, and the atmosphere wasn't conducive to writing. After about a month I moved back across the island to Santa Cruz, where I had already met a few locals through names given me by Tony Stubbing, who had spent some time there years before. These were chiefly native Canarians interested in the arts, who earned their livings at banks or newspapers or other mundane places, and their meetings were convivial affairs where only wine was drunk, though sometimes a good bit of it. This was mainly the local dry and brownish semi-sherry which I'm certain was the "canaris sack" esteemed by the Elizabethans. At these tertulias, as they were called, people would recite their recent poems and read from their novels or stories in progress and exhibit their latest caricatures or sketches or paintings, and so on. There was much good humor and singing of regional songs and discussion of esthetic matters, and often the gatherings reminded me of similar affairs in New York when I had been in Martha Foley's writing seminar at Columbia.

Several of the group were of the Civil War generation and their sympathies had been with the Republic, wherefore most had spent some time in jail. But the Canaries had been firmly in

Nationalist hands from the start—Franco was in command there when he launched his rightist rebellion—and thus had seen much less of the bitter bloodshed that took place among civilians on the Spanish mainland, where in franquista areas, when all the pent hatreds had been unleashed, such intellectuals as these had been butchered or forced to flee into exile, and were still absent. I had known some of their ilk in New York and in Mexico, and in Spain itself I had missed their presence.

Canarians were Spaniards and yet not Spaniards in a way. Most of them, even a good many rightists, resented the control exercised over the islands by Spain. They referred to peninsulars as godos, Goths, and felt strong kinship with Latin America, particularly Cuba—there had been much migration back and forth between Tenerife and that Caribbean island (then still under Batista's rule), and their dialects of Spanish were closely similar.

Thus Tenerife was a quite different experience for me from Mallorca. The ruling-class natives of Santa Cruz, so far as I could tell from my occasional contacts with them, were in some ways like their counterparts on the Mediterranean island—Catholic, protective of their privileged status, and judgmental in the manner that had so weighed upon my Lena. But their power and their political convictions had been weakened by New World influences, and by the survival among them of clots of humanistic freethinkers like those I came to know. These latter had no political heft at all—they were in fact still watched by the authorities—but socially they had their own separate weight. And the relatively few foreigners in the city, including me, were seldom lost souls, for most had interests and professions.

The novel seized me in its claws and did not really turn loose again while I was on the island, though there were fallow spells. Living at first in a Santa Cruz hotel and then in the upper floor of a house with a balcony above a park full of flame trees and laurels, I followed where the writing took me, glad to be really possessed by a piece of work. It had in it some of the best writing I had ever done and I knew this, and much dross also and I knew that too but believed that in revision it could be improved or deleted. I took its title, *A Speckled Horse,* from a visionary passage in the book of Zechariah that I still like:

> I saw by night, and behold a man riding upon a red horse, and he stood among the myrtle trees that were in the bottom, and behind him were there red horses, speckled, and white.
>
> Then said I, O my Lord, what are these? And the angel that talked with me said unto me, I will show thee what these be.
>
> And the man that stood among the myrtle trees answered and said, These are they whom the Lord hath sent to walk to and fro through the earth.

All my life I have been a sometime Bible-reader, even after the reverence that took me to the book in the first place had waned and changed. What has not changed is my reverence for its wording in the King James version, set down during a peak period of our language nearly four hundred years ago and having served during all that time, along with the Book of Common Prayer, as a reference point for linguistic eloquence and grace wherever English was spoken, even in backwoods places. And for me it is a matter for rage that contemporary pietists have managed to supplant its expression with their own pedestrian prose, in the name of "relevance."

I also fell in love on the island. She was a local girl named Consuelo, a skilled shaper of pottery who belonged to the little group of intellectuals and was another victim, like Lena, of the Spanish view of young women who had split with a novio and thus were no longer viewed as entirely respectable.

NOV. 30, PUERTO DE LA CRUZ: This is only my fourth day here, yet I've been moving, thinking, reading, writing. The place is not really what I expected—only a few foreigners in view just now and my setup is actually very lonesome, except for Jim and Lill down the way. But that is good too, for they take the edge off of the aloneness and I have time to read and think and write. It makes me do so. In the long run it may not be all that good and I'll possibly go live in Santa Cruz, but will face that when I have to. Am revising "EE. UU." and thinking of the novel.

Huxley, *The Gioconda Smile* (short stories), Lawrence, *The Woman Who Rode Away* (same), Michener, *Tales of the South Pacific*. The first two are generally first-rate with baddish patches. I do not envy either H.'s somewhat hollow intellectuality or L.'s feminine sun-worship, but I do envy them for getting their thoughts and feelings so freely into words. Michener to me at present looks like nothing at all—can't write, can't tell a story or even the truth, can't deal with complexity in characters, can only recognize good material and milk it.

[Old John: It did make a damned nice musical, though.]

Jim picks at me daily about getting on the novel. I'll get something done here. Can a change be slouching toward my Bethlehem to be born?

DEC. 4: Still going well, finished "EE. UU." in a burst of work and think honestly it's not bad. Jim likes it and is rather envious. He and his Lill—a fine girl but sad with the neurotic poison of competing with men, so that she reminds me in many ways of my Bryan. The same intelligent understanding and the same constant melancholy contemplation of her own inadequacy in a male world. And the same sucking at the energies of her man, and if that is what he meant when he said she was trouble, he was very right. I do hope things get better for them, because I like them both.

DEC. 6: *The Nigger of the Narcissus*—have read it before but in my way had forgotten it. Fine Conrad, the straight clean narrative of a rough voyage and its people. He never goes too inward but stays on the surface, letting the events themselves give you powerfully the feelings. A strong and monolithic book. Huxley, *Brave New World*—another reread, still good. He is much more concerned with ideas than with people, but with ideas he is unbeatable. W. H. Hudson, *The Purple Land*—I just looked through this one, reading parts. A romantic horseback journey through the Argentine pampas, with heavy reliance on atmosphere (though he knows that atmosphere well) and some occasional inconsequential love stuff. A good picture of a time and a way of life, but hardly a novel. I am certain that J. Frank Dobie was steeped in this book when he wrote *Tongues of the Monte,* for the framework and even some of the details are closely similar. William Sansom, *A Bed of Roses*—a quite bad new novel laid in Spain. In a plain prose sense it is excellently written, but it relies almost entirely on tourist information breathlessly presented, and the characters and plot are essentially soap opera, with a perversion at the end to try to take it out of the soap class.

In Texas a few years later, when I had come to know and love old Mr. Dobie toward the end of his life, I once mentioned to him the kinship I had thought to discern between his *Tongues of the Monte* novel, set in northern Mexico, and Hudson's *The Purple Land.*

Uncharacteristically, he clammed up and I knew I had been right.

DEC. 11: Have been working right along, finished the Swede story almost too easily and am not satisfied with it though it has much good. [This story was based on the death of my friend Swede Johnson in New Mexico, and became a passage in *A Speckled Horse.*] In part it exhibits my old defect of getting too lyrical with heavy subjects, and in part the trouble is that it is a segment of the book, with too much character and too many problems fitted into a tight space. It probably can be fixed but what interests me is the book. I will write it, starting here on this island.

DEC. 12: Final-drafted that story and it looks o.k., if somber as hell. Jim says it's the best thing of mine he has seen. He seems to be in a crisis in both his life and his work, and I don't guess I'm helping, dragging in my attempts at deathless prose while he is trying to finish a slick serial for *Collier's*. Probably he and Lill shouldn't have married, though it may work past these growing pains. To get out of the middle, where I possibly only aggravate things, I am thinking more and more of a house or apartment in Santa Cruz. If the weather is decent tomorrow morning I'll ride the bike over there and check around.

DEC. 18: [A long journal swatch on plans for the novel, of which there are many.] Jim being saddled with the alcoholic brother-in-law Norman. With all his foibles he is a very good man and takes on other people's troubles without thinking twice. He was willing to take on mine too but I am not the type to unload, and I discovered that this half-pleased but also half-disappointed him.

Have been thrashing around about apartments in Santa Cruz, without success but without worrying much about it. I've got my eye, for a change, on the work where it belongs and I'm going to keep it there. Maybe John (dare we say it?) is beginning to level out a bit.

DEC. 20: Santa Cruz yesterday, very agreeable, rooting around and knowing a few people, meeting likable intelligent Eduardo Westerdahl [to whom Tony Stubbing had sent me; he was an owlish little man, fifty or so, who worked in a bank and was immensely enthusiastic about Surrealist art, many of whose practitioners he had known]. I will move there after New Year's.

DEC. 23: Pepe's letter of great relief on hearing from me, for he had been worried. By God, he is a friend all the way. I've heard no more from Abe which bothers me because he may have been offended by my talking down our meeting. And day after tomorrow is Christmas, which rings pleasantly in the ear but means very little to me this year. At least it won't be as lonesome as some I've spent.

CHRISTMAS EVE: Old Norman is in the sanatorium over in Las Palmas for his Christmas, and Jim is swatting the brandy and Nembutal and not working and Lill is talking about divorce. I don't know what is the cause of what, though most of it is probably his frustration with the kind of work he has been doing and his fear of failure on the serious novel he's trying to get started on. Nor is Lill a help.

That was a bad holiday season that I will sum up briefly here. I was just an observer and glad of it. Norman escaped from the sanatorium and came back to Tenerife, careering drunkenly about and causing all kinds of trouble. Lill and Jim continued their wrangling and their progress toward a breakup. I played the Tomte, a kind of Swedish Santa Claus, and fooled at least little Lou-Lou, Lill's child. At a large gathering at the deluxe Hotel Taoro in the Orotava Valley, Jim and I nearly got into a fight with young upper-class Spaniards who were throwing tight-balled confetti in our faces; at another party Norman sneaked out and pulled the wires out of the car of another young upper-class Spaniard who was dating one of his stepdaughters, etc., etc., on into 1955, at which point I made my move to Santa Cruz.

JAN. 2, 1955, SANTA CRUZ: Over here yesterday, a wet trip across the high moors on the motorbike but well worth it. Into the loneliness of this hotel room, but the loneliness is getting to be something you can turn on and off like a light, which is all right if it keeps up. This novel may alight upon the American consciousness with the earshattering sound of a feather striking silk, but I think I'm going to write it. It is flowing—I woke at 4:00 a.m. to sit up scribbling for an hour and a half, and all morning I have been at it. These are all notes so far.

JAN. 3: Hart Pearson's farming—on 15 fanegadas [about 24 acres] he has approximately 5,000 artichoke plants, each of which bears six fruits a year. They sell at a shilling each in England, about four pesetas by the exchange here, making a gross of 120,000 pesetas or around $3,000, and the net involves subtraction of transport, labor, land rent, and so on. That would probably be a welcome return for an average local farmer, but it seems just dabbling for someone who in the States was making probably $20,000 or more. Maybe Dee-Dee has money. The peasants objecting because he won't put a cock in with the hens. The partridges he hopes to breed. The high sad fog-swept saddle there, misty and rich and gloomy. Celtic.

Hart P. was a tall, personable Midwesterner, a former Time-Life correspondent, whom I liked with reservations. He knew lots of people in Santa Cruz and was something of a womanizer, though he also had a semi-separated, attractive, very wacky wife called Dee-Dee who showed up from time to time with a small child. The mystery about his uneconomic farming, ostensibly aimed at shipping produce to England in the cold months, was cleared up for me later when Jim Phillips told me that Pearson was CIA and the farm was only a front. I suppose I should have figured this out for myself, but I never thought much in those terms.

The matter of various people's CIA connections cropped up often during my time in Spain. In truth the spooks were busy almost everywhere at that point, for the Cold War was in full bloom, and I myself was later invited to join up. One good friend of mine, Jim Phillips's youngest brother David, was a key CIA figure on the Latin American scene. . . .

JAN. 5: The way you pick up details about people gradually, many of them conflicting. This Tanya Tambelius, for instance, whom I've never seen.

(1) Jim in Madrid told me something about Caisa [Lill's sister] happening in when he was dancing with Tanya T. in pajamas, and I recalled that tale now because of the unusual and euphonious name.

(2) Jim says down here that she is a pretty good artist and he is helping her financially but can't talk about her around Lill. He also says Hart Pearson is interested in her.

(3) Hart says without admitting such interest that she is a really nice girl, very pretty, and it's funny how Jim has this benevolent kick and then loses interest after people get on their feet again. Says she is in Sweden for Christmas.

(4) Jim later, more specifically, says he is giving her 5,000 pesetas a month and has told her to just live and paint how and what she wants to.

(5) Eduardo Westerdahl today when her name comes up pricks up his ears, clearly quite interested. He says he knows her. I say that a friend of mine spoke of her.

Eduardo: "Uno alto, muy alto?" (That is very tall Hart Pearson.)

I say no, another friend of mine, in Puerto.

"Well," Eduardo says, "the alto is very interested in her. He is separated from his wife and wants to marry Tanya. She is really a stupendous girl."

I, knowing the alto has his wife here with him just now: "How does she paint?"

He thinks well—has seen only one tapestry design, interesting, and some pictures she is painting for an American group of whom he knows little. It seems this group is paying her 5,000 pesetas a month and requires that she paint only in a certain way, which she says is not really the way she paints.

"Oh," I say.

Eduardo: "Yes, and it must have been the Americans who put into her head the idea of opening a handicraft shop, with clothes and other things."

This was Pearson according to what he has told me. And on away from the reputedly beautiful and gifted and definitely cagy Tanya Tambelius to something of a gentle blast at Americans in general. A nice little guy, though, very warm and bright, and I liked his apartment crammed full of what seemed to me to be very good modern paintings.

[All Surrealist stuff, and I found out later he had been a friend of André Breton and had been instrumental in staging an International Surrealist Congress there in Santa Cruz during Republican times.]

JAN. 6, DAY OF THE WISE KINGS: A delightful wine-drinking supper and tertulia last night at La Laguna with a group of Eduardo's local friends—poets, prose writers, caricaturists, and so on. Discussion of literature etc. and then singing Canarian folk songs, and finally I gave them "All Around the Water Tank" and "Good Night, Irene" while playing someone's timple, a sort of regional ukulele. Very nice, and these are much more the kind of people I'm interested in knowing than the ones over in Puerto.

What I've got to do now is find a place in which to live comfortably, a good woman if any such shows up, some kind of regular exercise (maybe a rowboat?), and buckle down to this book. It is nearly time to start the actual writing, which I have been putting off in my mania for making notes and classifying them in separate folders etc. That is all largely necessary, though, given my unsystematic and forgetful mind, and I have needed this time for contemplation of the whole thing.

JAN. 7: With Westerdahl last night to a most pleasant Norwegian pork-and-akvavit supper at the house of one Knut Lagersvold. More songs, more timple-playing. Writers and artists and two handsome girls to enliven things, one of whom, the auburn-haired alfarera Consuelo, enlivened me considerably with a touching of fingers under an old dog's neck, and I have been thinking of her all of today. I.e., foolishness. The thing is they are such women when they are women.

Knut was an intelligent and moody fellow a little younger than I, who at seventeen had been lined up with a couple of friends in front of a German firing squad. The purpose was to make the boys spill information about the Norwegian underground of which they were a part, skiing in arms and information from Sweden. But they didn't talk, and weren't shot. This was something I found out from him later, for like me he had tried to put the war behind him. He was Norwegian vice consul in Santa Cruz, which meant mainly that he worked for the shipping company that sent fresh fruit and vegetables from the islands to Scandinavia.

Consuelo the auburn-haired potter, who had significantly entangled her fingers with mine as we caressed that fuzzy old dog, was to become very important to me.

JAN. 9: Today, following a house trail, I had tea with the most sympathetic Señora Bethancourt and we talked each other's respective ears off about Civil Wars and local gossip and such. Her late husband, the Masonic doctor, must have been one of the best of the old kind of freethinkers, and how they roughed him up. The woman who said, "El Doctor Bethancourt es como un padre a mis hijos, pero si le fusilan, bien fusilado está!" [The Doctor is like a father to my children, but if they shoot him, well shot he is!] And the local Falangists driving him down to the port in the dark to take him out in a boat so they could kill him "while escaping," and the dock grapevine spreading word and so many people showing up in protest that they were afraid to carry out the plan.

Consuelo's sexy little pots that have caused a scandal around here.

(Later) Some of the above-mentioned fascination waned after talking to Eduardo and finding out about the truly Scandinavian mess-à-trois that Knut has had with his Canadian fiancée and Consuelo.

JAN. 10: Began actually writing the novel.

JAN. 13: Am so hopped up I don't know if I can put down what it's like. This thing is dragging me with it. I am writing it and it is writing me. It looks beautiful. Ten damned years of trying are packed into it, and I thank God three times a day for having directed me through all the horsecrap to this point. This is what it was all for. I can't even sleep for waking up to write down passages, and then wake again at 5:30 to get up, twitchy-eyed, and hit it again. If this keeps up I'll be a physical wreck by the time it's finished, but I don't care. I'd take any kind of dope to get it finished. *I have never felt like this in my life before.* The Bird of Destiny is about to tear my God-damned shoulder off.

JAN. 18: Still moving along. A week of the euphoria, now calmer, but it is underway, conceived, and will go on.

My interest in the bright and lovely Consuelo did not wane for long. Even while the work maintained its grip upon me, we began to meet briefly every day or so in a café or a park, talking and feeling the current run between us, and I learned a good deal about her.

With the russet hair, green eyes, and pale perfect skin she had inherited from her late father, a ship's officer born on the north coast of Spain and lost in an Atlantic storm, she stood out among the generally brunet islanders and was sometimes addressed by Scandinavian or German tourists in their own languages. She had fallen in love with clay quite young, while still in a convent school where a nun had taught her the rudiments of shaping and decorating simple vessels. And later she had built an inner life around ceramics, evolving a very distinctive style with incised designs, occasionally abstract but usually representative in a somewhat Grecian manner, with scenes of animals and people that always had a humorous, often bawdy edge to them. Of these a Santa Cruz shop-owner would take as many as she would give him on consignment, selling them at good prices not only to tourists but to discerning locals. She had even had offers from abroad to reproduce her work in royalty-earning mass numbers, but had turned them down. That, she told me, would have taken away the pleasure of making them one by one, all varying slightly from the others even when the same design was used.

Just for pleasure, she also made and baked wickedly funny small caricature busts of red clay, representing various local personalities including members of the little group of intellectuals to which she belonged. She would bring the latest of these to one of the group's weekly gatherings, and would present it to its subject with a mock-formal speech. Later she made one of me, but did not show it at a tertulia and would not let me have it. . . .

Consuelo had left her very conservative novio because she had outgrown him, though she didn't put it that way. Intensely possessive, he had disapproved of her pot-making and of the friendships it created for her among the artistic crowd. Finally, fed up with his harping and tired of his ways, she had broken off the relationship, though he had never fully accepted the break but still lurked about at times and spied on her.

Her abrupt spurning of this formal link had shocked and alienated most of her Establishment friends, and if she had been living in another Spanish region, that kind of people might have managed to destroy her, as they would have destroyed Lena in Palma if given the slightest chance. But Consuelo lived in Santa Cruz, and had her blessed talent that gave her a place of refuge among those humanist survivors, who esteemed her for her work and for her brain.

Once when we were walking in a flowery park—Tenerife seemed to be always full of fragrant blooms—she gave a little leftward toss of her head without turning it, and said, "Allí! Allí anda Alejandro."

I glanced across, and from the next path over, sixty or seventy feet away, a broad-faced, well-dressed young man was staring at us between the tree trunks with an expression on his face that could have been hatred or could have been sheer misery. . . .

FEB. 10: Rode over to Puerto yesterday to visit Jim and Lill. I'm afraid he is a real rummy and I feel very bad about this because I like him. The only way he and Lill hit moderately contented stretches is via the old treacherous route of bottles and pills, and he is not working, because that seems to upset Lill by making her think of her own inadequacies. God, how we all destroy one another. He gave me a thoughtful criticism of what I showed him of the novel, and has genuine warm interest in it. But he is a real dark-night-of-the-soul type.

And the awful news from Faith in New York about Robert Cochrane and the subway train shook me. It was a logical thing for him to do—hell, I already had suicide mapped out for the character who is partly him in the book, which scared me—but it's very very sad.

And the little grupo of Spanish friends here, the older ones having been on the losing side in the big mess and still having to worry about politics and how they stand with those in power. Young Julio Tovar who is always going to write a prize novel and telling you all the details and diagramming the plot in pencil on a marble café tabletop. Domingo who wants to interview me for his newspaper, for God's sake. And the wondering about how they all feel concerning my relationship with Consuelo. Give the men tobacco and let the women alone, Hemingway said about getting along with people who speak Spanish, though I think he was quoting someone else. I can manage the first precept but evidently not the other.

Sliding for the moment past "the other," I will note that the tobacco available in the Canaries back then was superb and plentiful and cheap. It came in duty-free from Cuba, and premium cigars like Partagás and Gener sold for practically nothing, as did strong aromatic cigarettes from the same factories. In the reign of our present form of puritanism, I know it is abominably incorrect to admit to an affection for the genial weed, but in truth all my life I have loved it, and I loved it most of all in Spain. Even in Madrid the good Havana could be had in contraband four-hundred-gram dry bricks that crumbled into a consistency like that of Bull Durham. These I used to turn over to a rotund little lady who came by the Luxor every two or three days. On her next visit she would return it in "wheels" of fifty fat, perfectly hand-rolled cigarettes each, bound in rubber bands. This half-century later, when sound medical advice has caused me at last to quit smoking, I still look back with pleasure on the tobacco of those days.

As I do on the little grupo of Santa Cruz friends. Except for correspondence with Consuelo, I lost touch with them after leaving Tenerife, but they were an appealing, somehow innocent bunch of provincial intellectuals. Maybe it was in part my own subsurface provincialism that made us get along so well. Or maybe not—they remembered unprovincial Tony Stubbing with great affection, for instance, and were full of anecdotes about his ways.

The journalist Domingo Pérez "Minik"—his pen name—did publish a couple of brief pieces I wrote for him in Spanish, one on some pronouncement of Faulkner's as I remember. Another member of the grupo, whose name now escapes me, a shy humorous little man, drew wonderful cartoons. At the weekly tertulias Consuelo showed her new pots or busts. There were about fourteen or fifteen of us regulars, all told. I don't know if Julio Tovar, a chubby earnest young man, ever finished his novel—maybe he did before dying still young, for afterward Consuelo wrote me in America that a local literary prize had been established in his name.

A bulky man named Arístide Ferrer, one of those incarcerated during the Civil War, was an idealistic Socialist who was rich in local terms, from potato farming I believe. He was something of a puritan and disapproved of our drinking so much wine, but he came to some of the tertulias anyhow.

FEB. 12: Knut and his quite dumb Canadian fiancée Ellen and the enigma of that, unless he just wants the cash involved. And Mercedes the aging Norwegian consul's young Spanish wife and I can see a mess there from ten miles off, though it would be in a sense safer than this with Consuelo.

FEB. 15: Consuelo resolutely filling me in about her and Knut. He is a good boy, but troubled and at a crossroads, not knowing which way to jump, and I feel sorry for any woman who gets in his way at this point, as she did. I have been a little that way too, almost up to now, not now. And Ellen the pretty, wealthy, eternally immature, likely frigid fiancée, wondering ineffectually what all the stew is about.

By then I was living in the apartment above the little park with its laurels and flame trees, and Consuelo and I had become fully lovers, either meeting secretly there or going on the motorbike, she riding the pillion seat, to unpopulated pine woods that cloaked the sides of the Teide volcano, the island's most prominent feature.

In the apartment that evening, after love, she told me about herself and Knut. I knew the relationship had existed, but she said she needed to tell me herself about how she had taken up with him after ditching Alejandro and attaching herself more closely to the little band of artists and writers. Knut had been alone and loose at the time, and she had felt that way also.

"I suppose I did it to show myself I was free," she said. "I was never in love with him. I just wanted to erase Alejandro from my mind."

I said, smiling, "So Knut cured you of Alejandro, and now I'm curing you of Knut."

"No!" she exclaimed. "It isn't thus and you know it! You *saved* me from him. With us it is very different."

It was indeed quite different by that time, for we were deeply involved with each other. I wondered, though—without really caring—whether in the beginning it may not have been quite so different, for she had come to need liberation from Knut. He had gone on a long vacation to Norway, where he had met the Canadian girl Ellen, bringing her back to Tenerife with him as his betrothed. And in Nordic fashion he had been quite willing to continue relations with both Consuelo and Ellen, expecting them to like the arrangement and be friends, though neither of them spoke the other's language. Ellen was stupid enough to accept this in her eternally bewildered way, but not Consuelo. So that when I had showed up not much later and the electricity had flowed between our fingers under the neck of Knut's old dog, I imagine I had looked like a blessed happenstance to her, a solution.

But yes, it was different now. Oh different indeed . . .

FEB. 17: Jim called this morning and it seems they're busting up. It is sad even though I was expecting it. Much sadness is around just now. The letter from Faith about Robert and the subway train. Edkins' marriage and the sad fey letter about that. Sam Hynes wallowing in the graveworm aspects of

Donne and Marvell. But I'm not sad. It seems to me that I'm still floundering around ass-deep in mud, but am very close to the main highway for a change, where the footing is getting firmer.

Thus Tenerife, where I stayed for another couple of months, a productive and on the whole happy time. I kept working, and meeting with the members of Eduardo's tertulia, and seeing much of Consuelo, admitting to myself finally that I did love her and wondering about marriage. Jim stormed through Santa Cruz on his way out of the island and wrote to me later from Mexico City. Soon afterward Lill left too and we had a fond farewell.

I met the mysterious and, yes, beautiful Tanya Tambelius at one of the grupo's parties, but she was aware of my awarenesses about her and stayed on the other side of the room as much as she could. Later on, when she saw that I wasn't going to strew gossip around, we became friends, though she was a strange one, obsessively certain that the Russians were going to take over Sweden, unwilling to write to her husband who was imprisoned in Siberia, rebellious against Hart Pearson who had been directing her affairs. I never knew exactly what relationship existed between her and Hart, or between her and Jim Phillips for that matter. Balding, aging Eduardo Westerdahl, I knew, was wistfully in love with her. That might have been partly ethnic, for his father had been a Swedish seaman who had jumped ship in Santa Cruz to take a local wife and stay. Eduardo later married a bluff masculine Frenchwoman named Maude, the widow of one of his old Surrealist painter friends, also a Canarian, whose name I have forgotten but his nickname was "El Cocodrilo," the Crocodile.

I explored the island on motorbike trips, sometimes with Consuelo on the pillion, or often alone. I went high up the side of

Teide—"Padre Teide," a bawdy folk song called that conical volcanic height:

> *Tenerife está repleto*
> *De estranjeros y de godos.*
> *Levántate, Padre Teide,*
> *Y dales por el culo a todos.*

Tenerife is full of foreigners and Goths. Rise, Father Teide, and stick it up all their butts. . . .

At that altitude I could look out above mists across the ocean at the mountainous tops of the other islands in the archipelago. I threaded green valleys and crossed high moors, and went to beaches on the edge of the dry, almost desert eastern slopes where camels were still used as beasts of burden. Parts of the island, especially the high cloudy valleys with little silent stone villages, had a pervasive ghostly feel, and I used to wonder if this derived somehow from the aboriginal Guanches, whom the Spanish had not fully conquered till 1492, when Columbus used Tenerife as a jumping-off place for his first voyage to the unknown west. It was said that these natives had had no boats and there had been in their time no communication between the islands. Eventually the Guanches who had not been killed off while fighting the Spanish invaders had interbred with them, and among the rural folk I often noticed a distinctive cast of countenance about the eyes and cheekbones, which undoubtedly stemmed from that source.

I have a lot of other random memories of the island, a couple of which involve Scandinavians. One is of a time when Knut Lagersvold asked Consuelo and me if we wanted to go on an afternoon's cruise offshore in the Atlantic, with a group of visiting Norwegians. He himself had pressing business and couldn't come along. Accepting, we soon found ourselves afloat with a Canarian captain and six Nordics of whom two women spoke a little English, and one fleshy middle-aged man could use a sort of pidgin Spanish.

The boat was not a fancy craft, just a stout seaworthy tug that Knut's company used for bringing produce to Santa Cruz from remoter parts of Tenerife and from the other islands. It was pleasant seeing the isle and its volcano from out on the deep, very blue water. But the day was warm and nearly windless, and at one point the Nordics decided to go swimming and started peeling off their clothes and diving in. All but one, a younger blonde with prominent bell-shaped breasts, had looked quite a bit better when dressed. Before he dove, the pidgin-speaker, with gestures, indicated that the remaining three of us ought to join the fun.

The captain smiled and shook his head. "Hay peces malos," he said. There were bad fish. Consuelo, whatever she thought about the fish, was not about to expose her shapely body to the general view, and I declined also, for I was not only unused to being naked in public but had a memory of Pepe Mut's remark about "bichos gordos" on a similar day at sea.

The Norwegians swam and splashed and cavorted and called and laughed, and finally clambered one by one up a little rope ladder to the tugboat's deck, water streaming down from all their appendages. The pidgin-speaking man bellied up to our captain triumphantly: "You see? No bad fish!"

The captain held up an admonitory forefinger. "Ala!" he said, and went into the boat's small galley, emerging with a shiny tin coffee-can lid. He skimmed it a short distance out in the clear water and it began to sink slowly, swooping from side to side. When it was five or six feet down a shark at least twelve feet long, with two smaller ones following, darted out from beneath the boat and grabbed it.

"Tiburones," said the captain. "Bastante malos, no?"

Gasps and shouts and jabbering ensued, and the well-endowed blonde went into mild hysterics that required several shots of the captain's brandy, nor was there much joy aboard as we chugged back toward Santa Cruz. . . .

Another recollection is of a midday luncheon and drinking party at Knut's large apartment, in an old house with high ceilings and large thick oaken doors. All of the twenty or so people there were Scandinavians except for Consuelo, myself, Knut's Ellen, and two or three Canarian wives of Norwegians or Swedes.

None of these people were steady, daily drinkers like the expatriates on Mallorca. The ones I had known among them till then had seemed to be sober, responsible business types. But when they did drink, the lid came off. At each place setting at that luncheon sat a jigger of sesame-flavored, ice-cold akvavit, regularly refilled by servants, to be tossed off after each of numerous guttural toasts, incomprehensible to me, had been proposed. There was also dark beer for chasers. Course after course of heavy food—sweetened fish, game, fowl, and several dishes unidentifiable because of either their thick sauces or the tongue-deadening effect of all that alcohol—were brought in and consumed, and the skölling and the swilling never ceased.

Though I had a reasonably good head for drink, after a fair dose of this routine I started tingling and squinting my eyes. Consuelo, wiser, after one sip of akvavit for the first toast, had taken to pouring hers into a pot of flowers each time her jigger was filled and pretending to drink from it empty when another toast came along. Looking around, I noticed that most of the other women present, and two or three of the men, were faking too, and started doing so myself.

When the meal was just about over the Nordics were not speaking their toasts but yelling them, with one fellow wandering about on hands and knees underneath the long table, causing squeals among the seated ladies whose legs he stroked. Another was passed out on the floor in a corner, and Consuelo looked at me. "Me parece que ya," she said, meaning let's get out of here.

I agreed, and we went to where Knut was seated beside Ellen

at the table's head, to thank him and say goodbye. He said nothing but got up unsteadily and went with us toward the thick carved door of the room. Just before we reached it, though, he moved ahead and spread-eagled himself against it, facing us, his hand gripping the big brass door-handle.

"Not leave!" he said in English, very drunk, waving us back toward the uproar at the table. "Got to see party through all the way! God-damn American! Can't drink!"

There were undertones here, unleashed by the akvavit. He and I had come to be fairly good friends, but from time to time I had sensed in him an abiding resentment of the fact that I had, in effect, taken Consuelo away from him. It had needed doing, and for her it had been an escape from an impossible three-cornered mess. But for Knut it had meant being left with only the child-like Ellen who, however much money she might have, was a pallid contrast to this bright young Spanish woman I had come to love.

Knut sagged a bit where he stood against the door, but held on to the handle and regarded me with a sneer. "Yah!" he barked.

I have never been a very combative type and have nearly always walked away from that kind of trouble when I could do so without shame. But I heard Consuelo beside me let out a tremulous sigh, and I said, "Knut, I like you fine when you're sober. But if you don't get away from that door, you and I are going to have a damn big fight."

Our eyes locked and held for a short time before he dropped his gaze and slid sidewise from the door. I opened it and we left.

"El pobre," she said, shaking her head and blinking back tears. "El pobre de Knut."

I worried and wondered and often exulted over Consuelo until I left Tenerife. It was an intense relationship and she was the first woman I had been able really to love since Bryan years and years before. With dark-eyed Lena in Palma I had come close, but both of us had known our intimacy could last only briefly and had therefore held back from admitting fully, even to ourselves, how we felt about each other.

I thought often of asking Consuelo to marry me, and was restrained, just barely at times, by the knowledge that I still had a lot of proving of myself to myself to accomplish, and that marriage wouldn't be right till that was done. Nor was she the kind of woman who could be put on ice in the meantime. Nor, in truth, was I certain how comfortably a Spanish girl from the provinces might fit in wherever it was that I might end up.

But the restored capability for love was matter enough for exultation. In long and perhaps overanalytical (and definitely self-centered) retrospect, I think Consuelo was part of a healing and growing process, which was not necessarily as good for her as it was for me—though she did, not long afterward, marry an understanding local man, apparently happily, and had children whose photographs she sent to me in Texas.

Another part of that same healing process was the work I did in Santa Cruz and the impetus it attained. In the end it turned out not to be the real work, but it was leading me there.

I returned to Madrid in May, seeing friends including Pepe Mut, and going to all of the San Isidro corridas. The exchange at that time was such that even an impecunious type like me could afford two front-row barrera seats for all seven of these fights. At one of them I watched the single most lovely faena I had ever witnessed, performed by a slight, ill-favored Venezuelan named César Girón—a stroke of felicity since I have never seen any more bullfights anywhere after the ones that week. Before the kill, standing with his feet close together, he used the muleta in four separate, supremely confident passes full of grace, one behind his back, to bring a beautiful bull all the way around him, close, and his feet never moved. The kill was perfect too. Maybe all the good, bad, or indifferent corridas I had gone to in Spain, and the interest I had expended on that bloody art, were justified by my being able to have full appreciation of that one exhibition by Girón. Or maybe not.

The girl Charlotte, who attended these corridas with me, was so overwhelmed by this performance that she threw one of her red shoes out in front of Girón as he marched around the ring in triumph, holding up the bull's two ears that had been awarded to him. Smiling at her, he picked the shoe up and waved it, handed it to one of his peones, and marched on. There was awkwardness later when we went to his dressing room to retrieve the damned thing, for he had seen it as a prelude to romance. I was going to write a story about that incident, but never got around to it. . . .

Going then up to the north coast, I spent about three weeks nursing a mild sinus condition and catching trout from a clean, rushing little river, in the company of a genial piscatorial priest who used worms. Then, by prearrangement, I met Consuelo in Santander, where she had come on the ship of her uncle, a Cantabrian-born merchant captain. He was a strong-minded, cordial, rather innocent man who was puzzled by the fact that I spoke intelligible Spanish instead of the grunts and pidgin talk he had grown used to in foreign ports. He was not stupid, however, and I thought it possible that he was pretending puzzlement as a compliment to my linguistic ability.

"You must have had Spanish ancestors," he declared. "It has to be."

I couldn't think of any ancestors who had not been English or Scotch-Irish in origin, with maybe a Welshman or two thrown in. But then I remembered unfortunate Monte Cavitt's unfortunate older daughter, and said that well, I thought I might have some Mexican cousins.

The captain beamed. "Anda!" he said. "Ya te lo dije!" I told you so.

Consuelo and I had supper each evening with him and three or four of his officers in a bodega, a cellar with huge barrels along its side walls. It had very good white wine and cider, the best kind of hard-crusted bread, and various local dishes of which my favorite was a big bowl of steamed tiny coquilla clams served in their own broth with lots of red pepper, and eaten from the shells with toothpicks. These meals were pleasant, with good talk, much of it about nautical matters. But the captain, for all his innocence and cordiality, had a very Spanish eye on the two of us, and after supper Consuelo went back to the ship with the others and I to my little hotel.

Thus we had no chance to be really alone together, and maybe that was best. But it was a frustrated, lovesick interval lasting a few days, during which she and I spent much daylight time at a table in an almost deserted bar-café on a hillside above the harbor, sipping wine or coffee and talking.

Once I asked if she still had the clay caricature she had made of me.

"Por supuesto," she said. Of course. "I brought it with me on the ship."

"To give to me?"

She shook her head. "No. If I am not going to have you as a man, at least I'll have your image."

We had never spoken of marriage, though the thought of it had always been with us. Now that she had brought it up, I did speak of it, close to tears as I told her the reasons it wasn't possible for me at that point in my life.

She was near weeping too, but said, "I see why not, Zhohn. Yes, I do see. But, oh, it makes me sad!"

It made me very sad too. I even remember the name and the sympathetic round-cheeked face of the bartender there, who somehow discerned our troubles. Fernando Cueli . . .

. . .

Then her ship moved on, carrying her forever away, and I took a boat to London. There I stayed in the old Cavendish Hotel in Jermyn Street for nearly a month, trying to continue work on the novel, visiting people I knew, and making arrangements for the trip home. Finally I caught a merchant ship at Liverpool and disembarked in New Orleans on July 20, 1955.

The Cavendish itself probably merits a digression. It was a special institution that I had lucked into on an earlier trip to England. Having belonged to and been operated for many years by a mistress of Edward VII named Rosa Lewis, it still had most of the paraphernalia and customs of that era, including very good food and the latest in a line of foul-tempered Skye terriers, all named Kippy—there were little brick-sized marble plaques set into the outside front wall of the building in memory of each of his predecessors, with dates. Kippy lurked under ancient lobby furniture and dashed out to bite people's ankles, and the long-time habitués of the place conducted a game to see who could get in the most kicks on him without being detected by Miss Edith Jeffery, the present proprietress and a former employee of Mrs. Rosa's, from whom she had inherited the hotel. They even kept score on an unlabeled piece of paper tacked to a bulletin board.

These guests were a heterogeneous, mainly genteel lot—rich Americans who occupied the expensive suites in front, less prosperous ones like me who took eighteen-shilling rooms in the back, country gentry in town for a fling or on business, colonials, regimental officers on leave from the fighting with Mau Mau rebels in Kenya, and so on. Whether you could get a room there depended on whether Miss Jeffery remembered and approved of you. Writing ahead for a reservation did no good, for she was absentminded and forgetful. When I showed up this time from Spain (having written) she failed to remember me and said with a vague air of distress, "Oh dear, I'm afraid we're full." But after a little conversation recalled to her mind the fact that I had stayed there before and had gotten along with the other guests, she suddenly remembered that oh yes, maybe there was one room. . . .

They tore the Cavendish down a few years after that. The institution and its original owner were afterward fictionalized in a BBC series called *The Duchess of Duke Street.* Later still, in 1995 in fact, I ran across a 1964 book about the place, Daphne Fielding's *The Duchess of Jermyn Street,* which detailed Rosa Lewis's career more or less from the start, and reminisced fondly about the hotel, of which the author had been a devotee since the 1920s. Not really an edifying account, for the clientele over the years were mainly rather negligible, prankish, upper-class wastrels, and the tone of things was intrinsically quite snotty. I made a note after reading it that the men often reminded me of Evelyn Waugh's awful character "Boy" Mulcaster in *Brideshead Revisited.*

And quite possibly Waugh may have encountered the prototype for this character while observing the Cavendish, for he was, as far as I know, the first author to focus upon it in a book. His *Vile Bodies,* wherein he satirized the hotel and its habitués and its proprietress, presents the Cavendish as "Shepheard's Hotel" and the Rosa Lewis figure as "Lottie Crump." Waugh was never forgiven for this transgression by Mrs. Lewis or the place's regulars, not that I imagine this bothered him greatly.

On the other hand these wastrels were by and large of the patrician cannon-fodder sort who as junior officers perished quite willingly and voluminously throughout the British Empire in its heyday and in two World Wars, thereby justifying to some extent their existence.

JUNE 26, LONDON: Not working, I drifted out to see a couple of old American movies. One was *Destry Rides Again,* which I hadn't seen before and didn't like. The other was a truly ancient piece of corn called *The Sun Shines Bright* about a Kentucky town, with all the clichés they could possibly drag in.

They played "Dixie" and all the blacks grinned and touched
their forelocks and it was so bad it should have been funny, but
at one point I found myself with tears in my eyes. These were
not for the falsehoods on the screen but for the old reality they
corrupted. We had something in the South and now don't have
it any more. There was probably much less good than evil in it,
but it was ours. What little is left of the old may last my time,
but I doubt it.

[Old John: As I damned surely should have . . .]

JUNE 27: More sentimentality. I stumbled practically blind
into another movie because I could find nothing I really wanted
to see, and this one, for God's sake, turned out to be about the
United States Marines, and liberties in San Diego, and the
fighting on Saipan. Called *Battle Cry,* with an overlay of trite-
ness mixed in with some real truths, though the truth as always
with the Marines is (and was for the folks who made this film)
hard to handle because it overlaps with so much standard jin-
goistic crud.

And now, here at the hotel, when I set down the date to
write these lines, I realize that it is eleven years ago tonight
since I lay wounded and bandage-blindfolded in a hospital tent
on Saipan and held that Southern kid Marine's hand while he
died. Eleven years exactly, and can that be coincidence?

JUNE 28: Item, to show how hard I am working: Out of
"mierda" ["shit" in Spanish], in only thirty or forty minutes
of effort, I succeeded in shaping the following anagrams—
admire, I dream, raid me, raid 'em, Mérida, armied, and Reid
am, as in, possibly, "Mistah Reid am waitin' at de do', suh."

JUNE 30: Things are shaping up, if not especially in the work,
at least in externals—passage, baggage, etc. Edkins turned up,
is contemplating emigration to the States and with his new wife
pregnant, for God's sake. Andrew Monteith [a decent young

Britisher I had met through Sam Hynes]. Dinner at the Burtons' [he was one of the De Havilland engineers from the Luxor]. All the loneliness goes as it always does. An agreeable supper at this wacky hotel this evening, talking to Tom Busha [American architect, friend of friends], and then this Major David Campbell who is in Kenya with the Black Watch, amiably butchering Mau Maus, a process he described in good-humored detail. Was also in Korea and likes U.S. Marines. I thought he was typical patrician conservative military British though of a good sort, and then he came up with the fact that one of his best friends is a journalist who is vehemently pro–Mau Mau. It seems not to bother him or the friendship at all. He is at the moment the champion Kippy-kicker of the Cavendish. . . . Another guest, a South African from Natal, says that the big fight down there will be not between whites and blacks but between Boers and British whites. Named Campbell too, a cousin of the famous or infamous poet Roy Campbell, who fought in Spain on Franco's side when most other literati were enlisting, if at all, with the Republicans.

My attitude toward the book is better. Abe's and Charlotte's comments were both strongly favorable, and I guess I'll soon get on the final stretch. Maybe it is weak to seek the opinions of others about your own work, but the fact is you get to where you can't see it clearly after long immersion in it. And both of them are people whose judgment I respect—especially, yes, when that judgment is favorable to yours truly.

Am rereading Lowry's *Under the Volcano,* a powerful piece of work. His use of language is so immensely and poetically strong and so full of wry hard humor that you accept the poor old drunken Consul whole-hog as a heroic figure, or at any rate as a fully sympathetic one.

JULY 3: Touristing at the Tower of London yesterday, pleasantly. I wonder (others have too) at the way England and Englishmen have changed, how all that brawling, aggressive, ambitious, lustful, murderous, and yet beautiful mess can have been transmuted into people who can invent austerity and go around wearing bowler hats. Tony Stubbing must be much closer to the original model, and so are many Americans, including the dead-drunk soldier I saw being dragged into a hotel in Regent Street by his uniformed buddies, in broad daylight.

JULY 13, ABOARD THE SS *KENDALL FISH:* [A good bit about the novel, on which I had been working during the voyage.]

Yesterday we passed close by Flores in the Azores where Sir Richard Grenville lay. Got a little swacked with the ship's officers last night, and found out that I had replaced two Spanish girls they were counting on for material.

The West Texas lady aboard, with her somber little daughter (how often alcoholics' children are thus) and her suitcaseful of Chinese ivory carvings acquired in France and the sozzled look in her eyes from drinking in her cabin, has given up on me. I listened to her addled reminiscences for a day or two—shooting a .45 at road signs at night was one amusement she and her husband engaged in during courtship—then established a polite distance between us.

June, the English girl who married a GI and is going back to him now after a visit to her family in Bristol, confides to me that she is under siege by one of the ship's young officers named Carl, who is evidently a very aggressive suitor, though with me he is a mild and earnest fellow who tells me about the farm he has in Alabama and his wife and children. . . .

Reading among the few random books that are on board. *The Heart of Midlothian*—I believe the Old South's fascination with Scott was based quite as much on ethnic, religious, and moral identification with his world as on the much-hammered Gothic illusion. This un-Gothic story with a different dialect could have been written by an antebellum Southerner, about

his own land. G. Greene: *England Made Me*—not much. About
halfway between one of his "entertainments" and a serious
novel, rather mechanical characterizations, full of G.'s essential
hatred of people. They come out painful, with bad breath and
pimples, and you see no hope for any of them. So you don't give
very much of a damn. Pietro di Donato: *Christ in Concrete*—
only glanced through. The sort of thing they went wild for
back in the thirties—guts, blood, big tits, the beating heart of
the people. Marxist, defective in execution, and its style is a sort
of sustained lyrical hollering. What happened to Pietro in later
times? Maugham: *The Razor's Edge.* Not my first reading of
this one. Maugham skirting the perimeter of the great verities
for the edification of the bourgeoisie. His formula: an excellently told story with enough intellectual pith to compliment
the reader into thinking he is sharing in profundity. He must
have worked out such things deliberately, for he was capable of
more, as for instance in *Of Human Bondage.*

We docked at New Orleans, where I was met by my sister
Nancy and her husband Bob Wynne. His brother was a doctor in
the city, with a large house on Saint Charles Street, and we cele-
brated my homecoming pleasantly for a few days, in the usual
restaurant-and-Latin-Quarter fashion, before driving on to Texas.

SEVEN

Long Island and the Book

(1955–1956)

I REMAINED IN Fort Worth until late October, living at my parents' house, not getting much done on the novel, but engaging in a lot of fishing and hunting and such with old friends. Acquired a secondhand Studebaker and started wondering about the next place I would find in which to work.

SEPT. 10, FORT WORTH: Yesterday, at Walt's ranch, I did about as good shooting as I have ever done in my life—fifteen fast, dodging doves in a stiff wind with approximately a box of shells. They were coming in at a waterhole and I could hardly miss at times, and God was it fine!

Walt's story about his delightful old father's drinking. When it gets to the real binge stage, Walt starts going to early Communion every day, and the minister sends a daily postcard saying, A loved one is praying for your recovery from this illness, and the old man gets furious and quits, at least for then.

SEPT. 21: Reading. (1) Rabelais—I'm not sure I ever did really read him before, except to search out dirty passages when young. How surprising it always is when classics turn out to be what they're supposed to be. (2) B. Traven: *Rebellion of the Hanged* (Nancy's recommendation). The beginning of the revolt against Díaz in a lumber camp in southern Mexico.

Strong thirties-type revolutionary writing which piles horror on horror until, if he could make his people come more alive, you'd accept it all within its context. Undoubtedly overdone but legitimately so. It becomes a tract toward the end and he loses sight entirely of his characters. Weird, but frankly more than I expected from this writer. (3) Arturo Barea: *The Forging of a Rebel.* The one that Julio Tovar told me about in Santa Cruz. Sensitive writing about Madrid and a Castilian childhood, and the Civil War. He is so frank about himself that he loses stature, confessing cowardice and so on. You get to where you don't really like him but you still respect him. It is a good picture of the intrigue and confusion among the Republicans in that war, quite a bit different from the single-minded, happy People's Army idealized by many foreign observers, e.g., Robert Capa. (4) Claude Bowers (an ambassador back then): *My Mission to Spain.* Standard New Deal liberalism with much rote thinking, but it also has a lot of good information in it, especially regarding the north-coast phases of the war, the personalities of leaders, and so on. (5) José Antonio de Aguirre: *Escape via Berlin.* The Euzkadí president, clearly honorable and very Basque. That was lost too, and it was possibly the only part of Spain with people sturdy and independent and cohesive enough to make representative government work. Maybe that's the only way it can work right, in smallish geographical units, with personal contact, ethnic homogeneity—the Jeffersonian thing. (6) Arthur Koestler: *Dialogue with Death.* First-rate. A consistent clearly difficult balance between objectivity and his own liberal sympathies. Covers his experiences at the taking of Málaga and in a condemned cell at Seville, and it boils down finally to an excellent short prison memoir. There is an extreme modern preoccupation with himself—his hurts, fears, physical state, reading, smoking—but it is combined with a powerful genuine sympathy for the suffering of others, though that seems often (is this fair?) to be an extension of his own sensitiv-

ity into them, plus a guilt for not *being* them, the poor and the
humble who are sent to the firing squads while he continues to
be spared. But K.'s kind of objectivity is rare in those who were
writing about that war from close up. A gifted writer and a fine
unpretentious book.

All the epistolary uproar in *Time* about their praise of Her-
man Wouk's "normalcy" in a long review of *Marjorie Morn-
ingstar.* How Mencken would have chuckled to see the
booboisie rising up to praise the man who tells them they've
been right all along. It is as if they have been suffering silently
through all of modern literature, made to feel queasy about
their gross ways and values, in order now to be able to rise up
and cheer wildly when one writer tells them that they're vindi-
cated and the other stuff was a big mistake.

OCT. 1: Was it by this date that you were to have finished the
book?

OCT. 4: Reading Bedichek, *Adventures with a Texas Naturalist.*
A very pleasant hodgepodge. I suppose all nature writers in
English are influenced by the same British models in terms of
form—White's *Selbourne,* Lord Grey, etc.—which in some
hands is a license to have no form at all. Bedichek shares many
of my own prejudices against nature-destruction and artificial-
ity, but surely he needs to smile when he says that seeing the
vermilion flycatcher for the first time is a major event in one's
life. It might even be true, but the smile would help.
Altogether, however, he is an even-tempered, sadly amused
man of intelligence, taking himself a little seriously, but don't
we all?

OCT. 7: The way a clean north wind, after all the sticky lack-
adaisical heat around here, seems to blow your head clear. I was
alone in the old Green farmhouse down at Walt's ranch and the

hawks came through in migration, one great swirling whirlpool of them after another, drifting south on the wind. There must have been three or four thousand in all, of several buteo species.

Then I drove the Studebaker to New York, seeing friends along the way, and ended up renting a house on the shore of Long Island's Peconic Bay, next door to Alex and Gina Brook's Sag Harbor home. There I worked quite hard most of the time, finishing by early May a retyped draft of *A Speckled Horse,* 441 typescript pages, though I could see that it still needed drastic revision.

Increasingly as it had built up, the novel had become a full-fledged bildungsroman, with sections on the protagonist's Texas background, his war and his postwar thrashings, New Mexico, a brief bit of New York, and much of Spain. He was very close to being Young John Graves, that protagonist, though with embellishments and some subtractions—being, for instance, an academic rather than a writer.

Sag Harbor was a good time in good surroundings and with good friends nearby, and the work mainly flowed along, with some periods of block. Few distractions beyond Alex in his more Russian periods, and a spirited, intelligent, finally a bit demanding lady from down the Island, and, in the spring, fishing which has always been and remains to this late day a distraction I seldom resist.

The artistic crowd—though not yet the teeming celebrity element of today—had begun to establish themselves out there in the erstwhile environs of the Bonackers and the New York rich, and I met some of them including Jackson Pollock, but did not enter their world.

Occasionally I drove into New York and visited around with old friends, becoming especially close with the artist Harry Jackson whom I'd met and liked in Madrid; he had a loft-studio on

Alex and Gina Brook

the Lower East Side and was having trouble with his second
wife, a high-strung modern dancer.

There was also a group of Texans who assembled often at the
Oyster Bay home of Wallace and Florence Pratt, he being a
Houstonian and one of the early heart surgeons, an avid com-
petitor in both his profession and the racing of sailboats—so avid
that I tended to shy away from crewing for him, though I liked
him very much. Sailing with Wally, even when there was no
race, was a straining to get the most out of the boat, with no time
for simply basking in the pleasure of the water and the wind and
the day.

The friendship with Alex and Gina got better and better—he
was a moody and demanding and cantankerous old bastard
much of the time and I got fed up with his self-centered ways on
occasion, but I loved him.

NOV. 3, SAG HARBOR, N.Y.: Nearly a whole month of fishing, traveling, visiting, thrashing, ending for the time being
here. I should have had this journal out, making notes along

the way, with Arkansas and old Dr. Barcus and the guide and the big bass I caught, then Saturday night at the country club in Nashville with the Derryberrys, then Swarthmore seeing Sam Hynes.

NOV. 4: I rather like it out here on the Island, even aside from the pleasure of being with Alex and Gina. May settle down and take the little house next door. The city is better in terms of women and multiple friends and all that, but unless you have more money than I it entails a lot of grubbiness.

NOV. 15: Settled here now in the little house on the bay. [It belonged to the widow of a painter friend of Alex's named Niles Spencer, well-known like Alex back in the 1920s and '30s.] It was the right thing to do. If I can keep from getting too lonesome, especially for women, I will get a lot of writing and reading and thinking done here this winter.

Pleasant drive back from New York with Alex the other night, lightly sipping Jack Daniel's all the way. Much friendly philosophy, and when we got here he issued a blast about contemporary painting, a protest against meaninglessness and impermanence. Some of it could be the bitterness of an old man superseded, but not all. He has dedicated himself to his art and not whorishly.

NOV. 17: [Some grousing about getting back to work on the novel.]

Reading: Robert Coates, *The Farther Shore,* a rather beautifully done piece on the breaking down of a lonely man in the city. Lacks stature somehow, has dull stretches, too analytical and talky where action would often serve better. I too run that risk. Gertrude Stein, *The Autobiography of Alice B. Toklas:* An impressive old girl who had the sense of Destiny in excelsis, perhaps with justification. She knew practically all the good writers of her time, impressed them, and helped form some of them. What a good time it was, everyone knowing everyone else and being alive and circulating around and interested, and where did it all go? One war awakened it, really, and the Depression plus another war finished it off. Maybe it came from being able to regard the laboratory chaps in thick glasses as inferior, maybe from an incomplete vision of the hopelessness? Styron, *Lie Down in Darkness:* Only glanced through this one and don't want to do more than that for the moment, because it would likely mess up my own work. It looks very good, based on an intense introspection which is not my way—but which, reading, I might be liable to think *ought* to be my way.

Something worth copying from Gertrude:

No, she replied, you see I feel with my eyes and it does not make any difference to me what language I hear, I don't hear a language, I hear tones of voice and rhythms, but with my eyes I see words and sentences and there is for me only one language and that is english. It has left me more intensely alone with my eyes and my english. I do not know if it would have been possible to have english be so all in all to me, otherwise. And they none of them could read a word that I wrote, most of them did not even know that I did write. No, I like living with so very many people and being all alone with english and myself.

One of her chapters in *The Making of Americans* begins, "I write for myself and strangers."

Me too, at least when I'm writing honestly.

Alex's parents, Georgians who came over to New York in 1886, had six children of whom he was the youngest and the only male. Poor but cultured, good parents. They came from that region where the long-lived people are, and one of A.'s grandfathers reached 115. A. when young drew with chalk on slate washtubs in the kitchen, pasted pieces of paper with pictures on them under the dining room table, watched his mother cook. Russian ships' officers (that was still in tsarist times) would visit his parents sometimes or invite the family aboard their vessels to eat caviar. Polio stopped his schooling after the sixth grade, and his only subsequent education was at the Art Students League later on. Always loved books, however, and is really quite well-read. At the moment he is painting frolicsome bawdy nudes and such, just for fun: "You know, one thing I am is a hell of a fine draftsman."

One of his sisters, now in her eighties in a nursing home in the Midwest, gets bored in the evenings, climbs out a window and over a fence, and goes to a bar to drink and make friends.

Gina had a standard, prosperous, boring East Coast marriage to a stockbroker but wanted to paint. One day she packed a suitcase and got on a train to Santa Fe, changing her name en route, from Virginia back to her childhood family nickname.

F. M. Ford, *The Great Trade Route:* Old Fordie being irascible about Norths overwhelming Souths. Pleasant and arbitrary and mostly wishful thinking—of my own sort, of course. It is rather weird to have thought out certain things for yourself and then to find out that someone like this has done it before you— the course of human history being decided by Pickett's charge at Gettysburg, for instance. I rather wish Ford had lived on for me to know him, as for instance I know Alex. He is someone I think I would have sought out and introduced myself to, as I have not wanted to do with others—Robert Graves on Mallorca, for one, or Hemingway at Pamplona.

V. F. Calverton, ed., *American Negro Literature* (an anthology, as of circa 1929): Much complaining, much myth-making about the Negro who (did one ever, really?) got back at the whites on their own terms. One quite special character named George Schuyler, a sort of black Mencken, who points out the follies of all this. Maybe, as Gertrude Stein says, the trouble with the blacks *is* nothingness, though that's not their fault.

NOV. 22: The solitude is beginning to show its value. Of course, by now you've learned how to waste time alone better than with others, but aloneness still has some good effects if you cut yourself off from hunting and fishing and such. And all this note-making, paper-staring, and thrashing has its function as a preliminary phase, since I've laid off the work for so long.

Last night I made a horrible dent in the considerable mouse population of this house, a hitherto carefree and happy crowd. Caught eight finally, going each time I heard the clack of a trap to reset it and dump the corpse, and I feel a bit murderous. But they have been crapping all over the drainboard and elsewhere.

NOV. 29: Rereading last night, backward and forward and without really intending to, Budd Schulberg's *The Disenchanted*. What's wrong with it? It is good reading and not shallow. In one of Thomas Mann's essays he says that what makes one work of art stand out from others is its sympathy. This one even has that, but it gives me the feeling of only another topical novel. Part of it is perhaps the inevitable consciousness of the difference of its protagonist from the real-life model, who was Fitzgerald. Much of that part reminds me of Jim Phillips, too.

Am wondering about the French novelists and whether they are not bad for us—all that logic piling up page after page and character after character, subjugating everything to an overt meaning. The Anglo-Saxon and Russian geniuses are different and bigger and better, though certainly sloppier for the most part. But so is life. Will have to reread Flaubert, Stendhal, etc., and actually read Proust, which I have never really managed to do. I am beginning to think that Bryan was right about *Madame Bovary* being dull. I think it bored me too if I'd had the guts to admit it.

So many things I ought to remember. Sunrise, for instance, from the balcony of the Residencia Príncipe in Santa Cruz, with the flame trees below and Grand Canary shouldering up through fire-edged storm clouds to the east, and Destiny sitting heavy on my shoulder.

A. Whitney Griswold, president of Yale, says that you cannot prohibit ideas, that the only defense against them is better ideas. This, of course, is based on knowing the Truth and having it make you free, etc., and implies that if a system finds certain ideas dangerous it means either that the ideas are right, or that something is wrong with the system. This is probably crap; systems have to defend themselves. My own notion is that what the individual must decide is whether, for him, a given system is worth defending. The one I see around me now is, for me, worth neither defending nor attacking. It has a sort of inevitability about it.

DEC. 2: Forty pages of Part III as of yesterday. Am not burning up the Smith Corona but am moving fairly steadily and it is taking on a little shape.

Skipping through Wolfe's *Of Time and the River*. His continually maintained state of excitement and raw-edged receptivity is hard, at my age, to take. And the long, absolutely faithful, embarrassing conversations, and the way he will not let an emotion hit the reader starkly and with single power, but must immediately start foaming and then worry it through many pages. There is much acute observation but it gets lost in the shouting. There is real poetry, but the fatigue induced by the rhetoric that precedes it keeps you from rising to it. . . . Maybe I'm just not in the mood for old Eugene Gant.

[Old John: Nor was I ever in that mood thereafter. I think you need to come at Wolfe quite young.]

DEC. 5: A party at Eleanor Stierhem's in Setauket last night, and damned if old Electric Boy didn't go to work again, exchanging sparks with a slim, bright, young advertising lady, and wasn't it nice?

I will finish this book and revise it this winter, maybe even well. Perhaps this girl Paula will carry me through the last of it as Consuelo carried me through the first part. You damned leaning tower. Maybe I am, but less of one than most.

The affair with Paula did turn out to be supportive in that way, and kept me from fretting about women during the winter and spring. It was a lighthearted relationship in the beginning, not at all deep and involved like the one I had had with Consuelo, and neither of us wanted it to get too serious. An intelligent, humorous, well-educated person, blonde with a classically Anglo-Saxon face—somewhat medieval, really—Paula was, like many advertising people, infatuated with language (why else would she have taken up with an unestablished writer?) and had once had literary aspirations of her own. She lived down the Island and worked at an agency in the big city, and we visited back and forth on occasional weekends during the whole time I lived in Sag Harbor. In the end, though, she was not the casual lover that she thought she wanted to be, and did grow serious.

Maybe I was simply not drawn to hedonistic women, or they were not drawn to me. . . .

DEC. 25, EVENING, FORT WORTH: This Christmas season at home is more or less as usual, though I'm not really feeling so out of place as in other years that I remember. I have a softness toward this hometown now, born I think of the knowledge that it can no longer touch me, really.

[Nor could it, even though I moved back there later and have lived not far away ever since.]

JAN. 14, 1956, SAG HARBOR: Back here a few days ago, after too long away, and was glad to return, even after the very good quail hunting at home. Have to go now through the whole process of working up steam again.

Am loaded with fishing fever, making up a fiberglass fly rod and putting in big orders to Herter's for fly-tying materials, etc. May branch into spinning tackle too, here on salt water. All this is not good for the writing.

I think the north coast of Spain comes closest to being the place for my "house on a mountainside" that I used to dream about. Maybe later I can own one there, for summers, near a pretty trout river. . . .

JAN. 17: And, I having refused to go into New York with Alex yesterday on the grounds that I would lose a couple of days' work, he made me lose them anyhow by (1) coming over here yesterday afternoon with a bottle of Cutty Sark, and (2) showing up at 11:00 today with a demand that I go to Southampton with him for oysters. What it amounts to is that he's not getting any work done and therefore by God nobody else is going to either. But I do have much love for the old curmudgeon. Gina, who has coped with his ups and downs and rages and euphorias and depressions mainly by creating a sort of haze around herself, says that their path is strewn with friends discarded by him. If this keeps up, I'll be another such, because I'll blow up at him. I *have* to get to work.

Reading Turgenev, *Fathers and Sons*. How the hell you missed books like this earlier. They're probably as good or better for me now, however. Technically old T. is tremendous— has the advantages of the Victorians like multiple viewpoints and wandering around when he wants to. But he never abuses these privileges, always telling his story concisely and well. Beautiful detail, especially of manners and so on. Russia was in the big transition we still haven't finished, and T. was clear-eyed, maybe rooting a little for the new but seeing the good things about the old.

You—I did, anyhow—end up feeling relief when Bazarov dies. I think Turgenev did too. Bazarov is Tony Stubbing. Gina said this, one of those intuitive insights she has. I didn't know she had observed Tony that closely. Even Bazarov's father and Tony's father are alike in the fascination they feel toward their sons, who in turn view the fathers almost with contempt.

And yet, looking back after many years, Old John is aware that there was far more to Tony than that—much warmth and fire and humor and capacity for friendship of his own variety. He was a part-time Bazarov, yes, but Bazarov only occasionally predominated in his viewpoint and his actions. In terms of women, though, he may have been more full-time, and that was most likely the basis for Gina's comment.

JAN. 18: The Bazarov business again: It hangs on in my mind through a consciousness of certain people who have in a way rebuffed me, whom I have wanted to be closer to, but with limited success. The only two recent ones I can think of are Tony Stubbing [but see Old John's demurrer above] and Eva Flores, totally different people but alike in their fierce standing alone, and in their rather scornful use of other people. That makes rejection by them, if you can call it that, a bit less personal, for I can't think of anyone they have fully accepted. They don't need other people, or perhaps are afraid of needing them. And I to others, God help me, have sometimes been the same, even if not as extremely or consistently. Think of poor Cochrane. Think of quite a few women. . . .

JAN. 20: Slowly edging into the work again. Am snowed in out here, can't get the car up the driveway to the road, and it's odd how little difference it makes. Can walk across the bridge for groceries. Snowed in is not a bad feeling, anyhow for the moment. Haven't called Paula in a week and a half, since the last time I saw her.

Read some Russian short stories, chief among them Gogol's "The Cloak" (or Overcoat), out from under which so many moderns crept, as someone has said. It is old-fashioned with its moralizing and fantasizing ending, which could be chopped off, but the whole is powerful nonetheless. Poor old Akaky Akakyevich Bashmachkin. We have all known him. I for one, a little, envy him.

Alex had a kind of minor stroke last night, suddenly leaving our conversation for space, though he said later that he had retained awareness of Gina and me. It scared me a little. Him too.

A thought: Nick Adams also crept out from under Gogol's overcoat.

JAN. 25: [A passage complaining about the slow progress of my work, one of many such then and before and afterward.]

Read Smollett, *The Expedition of Humphrey Clinker.* It is sentimental, and so contrived in plot as to be transparent, yet it has the real glow of that older world I would have liked better, and the feel of its people.

A woman character for a story perhaps—highly virtuous, but in terms of things she did *not* do. E.g., my esteemed ex-wife. Is that fair? Yes, in part.

FEB. 3: Dismal weather that ought to be good for the work, but isn't at the moment. I am within one good thrust of finishing, if I can get around to that thrust.

Until I bathed today and started straightening things out in the house, I was getting to be like one of those Gogol or Turgenev bachelor country gentlemen who sit around in their dressing gowns, reading and thinking and letting their estates and peasants fall into disorder. Sat up last night till 4:30 reading Dickens, *Our Mutual Friend,* a vast Victorian tapestry of a book. Let her rip was the principle, and the competent drafts rolled out in monthly installments.

FEB. 10: After four days in NYC for better or worse, and of course no work done. Saw Harry Jackson, who turned out to be even warmer and brighter than I remembered. He is changing his whole style of painting and is confident though broke. Told some wonderful stories about war, cowboying, the art world.

Jackson keeps a photograph from "our" war of a very young and very crumpled and very dead Marine lying in a ditch, with his rifle. He showed it to me and tears came uncontrollably into my eyes and if I'd kept looking I would have wept. Old attachments and passions and sentimentalities die hard.

Jackson's studious tour of European museums, in progress when I had met him in Madrid, had led him into returning to realistic depiction, and in New York at this point he was painting scenes and people of the section surrounding his Broome Street loft on the Lower East Side. He was one of the very few non-Italians in that staunchly ethnic neighborhood, but his genuineness and vigor and charm caused its people, even the minor mafiosi who ruled it, to like him and accept his presence. They became quite proud of him after *Life* magazine, fascinated by his defection from Abstract Expressionism, ran a multi-page spread on his current painting, including a reproduction of his largest canvas, which showed a corner café where the neighborhood's aged patriarchs were assembled, sipping wine and regarding their portraitist. After that, as a sign of their esteem, the mafiosi put him on the list of the favored few who received an entire stalk of bananas whenever a fruit boat docked....

I started staying with him in the loft when in the city. We talked and read the King James and Milton and Shakespeare aloud to each other, and had many arguments. After one of these had turned a trifle bitter (I don't recall the subject), Jackson stared at me solemnly out of his round blue eyes and said, "I guess you and I are pretty damn different."

"Yes, by God, we are," I said.

"But, you know, we've got one great big thing in common."

"What?"

"Way back behind everything else," said Jackson, "way down at the bottom of things where nobody can see it, neither one of us gives a big shit."

That ended the disagreement. Several decades later, I don't believe his statement was true of either of us, especially him, but maybe it made us feel macho together.

Afterward, when I had moved back to Texas, Harry returned to his own Wyoming roots and became one of the best "Western" sculptors, highly prosperous during the years when the market for such work was booming, with his own foundry in Italy, a studio and ranch in Wyoming, and a sales office in New York. In the late 1970s my wife Jane and I went up to Cody one July for the unveiling of his statue of Sacagawea at the Buffalo Bill Museum, a large whingding with a senator, rich Eastern-born ranchers, and other bigwigs in attendance, and much partying.

There in Cody it was clear that Harry had begun to take himself much more seriously than he had in Europe and New York, and that in regard to matters Western he had come to see himself as an ultimate authority, more or less a voice from on high. (So much for not giving a shit . . .) He had an entourage of employees and hangers-on who treated him with as close an approximation to reverence as was possible in Wyoming. I still cared about him, but the change bothered me when I remembered the bright, inquiring, and flexible individual, alternately earnest and humorous, that he had been during the earlier stages of our friendship.

And when, two or three years after the Cody affair, his voice from on high roared in condemnation of the moral tone of an appreciative but objective essay on cowboys I had written and sent him for comment, the friendship perished in a clash of angry letters—though in recent years we have had two or three fairly amiable telephone talks, always with remembrance of that disagreement in the backs of both our minds.

The trouble was, I think, that the cowboy myth had become

for him a sacred thing that had strengthened and sustained him during a stormy and zigzag life. And he didn't want to see any aspect of it called into question.

FEB. 12: A moving story tonight from Gina about Alex and a pair of wirehaired terriers they had. The female got maimed and he had her put away even though she was only crippled. Then he and the male got to where they couldn't stand each other, so he made Gina have that one put away too. There had been other such things before. Probably because of his own lameness, she thinks, he can't stand imperfect creatures, and I think this probably has bearing on what he said to me about a friend's very imperfect widow, once a lovely and thoughtful person but now depressed and alcoholic, who telephoned him frequently to discuss her social and physical afflictions: "I wish she was dead!"

FEB. 16: A good week, all in all; the work has waked up, nine good pages in a couple of days—not much, but o the difference to me.

Paula has gotten herself involved and is happy and unhappy about the involvement by turns. I am not involved, seeing what is between us as an interim thing. I feel a little bad about this even though I did make everything clear from the start, and she herself said she wanted no long-term links. It is coming to me that a major difference between me and the great lovers and cocksmen of the world is that I see women as people.

Gina invited me to supper tonight and then called it off, Alex having evidently objected. It is possible that he's reacting against me as she says he has against so many others. When I bring my emotions on this subject into the light, I find that I give less of a damn than I previously would have supposed. Whatever his undoubted gifts and charms, he is a most wearing character at times and I get fed up with the way he treats Gina, and with being the buffer between them.

Once after a tantrum of Alex's had culminated with his stomping out of the living room, I told Gina that if she were twenty years younger I would take her away from him. She was delighted with this and later told Alex about it, which made him furious all over again. . . .

FEB. 21: Finished *Anna Karenina* last night, a rereading after a good many years. If a novel is supposed to be a picture of a society then this must be a damned nearly perfect one. Scope, understanding, richness. It is old-fashioned in the sense that a woman is punished for her sins, but the fact is that if a woman believes in sin she will be thus punished.

MARCH 3, NEW YORK: In town for a break. Influences on me, if anyone ever asks: Joyce because even people who haven't read him write differently nowadays because of what he did with English. Hemingway because any American who reads him is forever after infected with his virus. Faulkner because to an extent he defined my people, and has come closer than any other American to real tragedy. (Closer than Melville? Yes, for me.) F. M. Ford because at his best as a storyteller he is Henry James with cojones, and besides was willing to think for himself. O. Henry because as a kid I read too much of him. The Russians, especially Tolstoy. Shakespeare and the King James, which are always mentioned by the hacks? What speaker of English was ever not influenced by them? You breathe them. Mark Twain a little, certainly.

MARCH 5, SAG HARBOR: Back here charged up like a battery from the change and from talk with Abe, who likes the work I've done God bless him, and with Jackson, who has much of the same drive and interests as I, so that we rub off well on each other. Saw old Claudio who is upset over leaving the Church [it was not liberal enough for him], and Paul Field with his little Italian Marilyn Monroe girlfriend, with whom he is much happier than he was with the moody dour wife he used to bring to Pete's Tavern. Schaffner a bit titillated over gossip concerning me and Paula, passed on I guess by Eleanor.

Also Mike Cooper, who has TB. It is logical—frail as he is in the first place, eating nothing, smoking like a stack, ridden by guilt and inadequacy, painting his magazine illustrations and 25¢-paperback covers in a windowless hole of a basement. Poor guy, he got loose from old Ethel in Mallorca, but not from his own black dog. I at least have preserved the illusion that integrity is possible, but he hasn't.

What you've been doing will make a book, John, so on with it. I have to either go to Detroit with Alex later this week, or talk my way out of it.

Alex wanted to go there—and eventually we did so—to look at an available "Brewster Ford" with a basketwork body, classic cars being one of his many passions. His main car at that time, in which we would drive to Detroit, was a well-preserved 1939 Rolls closed in the rear but with an open chauffeur's seat that had only a canopy and curtains for use against rain and cold. He also possessed a 1915 Model T Ford with a gleaming brass radiator and fittings, given to him by the actor Robert Montgomery, who had married into New York society and owned a house in nearby East Hampton. Montgomery, a very likable if slightly pompous man whom I had known in California during the war, worshiped old Alex, and Alex made fun of him and mooched from him mercilessly. The "Brass T," a product of that mooching, ran beautifully and was lots of fun to drive through the Long Island countryside because you sat up high in the open air and could see over hedges and brush and fences.

MARCH 8: Two good days' work behind and now I've bogged, tying flies and so on. But it will pick up and move. I managed to put Alex off for a week on the Detroit journey.

Mann, *Buddenbrooks.* A Hanseatic *Forsyte Saga.* Not as good as I remember *The Magic Mountain.* You know Germans better after reading it, at least Germans of that dynastic mercantile kind, and I suppose that is one test of quality. But for me a rather hollow book, touching the surface of many things but going deeply into few, leaving irritating strings hanging.

Turgenev, *Smoke.* An extended short story or perhaps a prototype of what novels later became. Not nearly as strong as *Fathers and Sons.* Avoids the tragic ending it probably ought to have, whereas I am not certain that *F&S* ought to have the particular tragic ending it does have. Am getting a little tired of reading translated works in half-Victorian prose, but think it is likely good for me, stylistically, at the moment, since there is no danger of contagion. Like Gertrude Stein being so cozily alone with her "english."

MARCH 13: Feeling sort of devitaminized, a species of bachelor's scurvy from sitting around here without much exercise. But am intermittently plugging through on the work.

Consuelo is getting married, it seems. This is all to the good, for I know now—perhaps knew all along—that she was not for me. Yet still when I think of marriage, as one does think, I think of it in terms of her. The house on a trout river in an Asturian mountain valley, with big chestnut trees all around, and a snug room to work in, and her standing in the doorway . . .

MARCH 25: Reading all last night—it was daylight when I finally went to sleep—Mizener's book on Fitzgerald. It adds up to what F. himself said about Gatsby, and Dorothy Parker said about him: "You poor son of a bitch!" And yet there are F.'s books—if you can distill that sort of thing out of your messes you have largely justified them. F. at my age thought himself old, and that "emotional bankruptcy" notion of his ruined and killed him and yet was all untrue. He wrote better and better all the time. This book has a picture of him at two and a half years of age with a wooden rocking horse, holding a whip. Shortly after that he began using the whip on himself rather than the horse, and kept it up till he died. Having a lot of fun along the way, of course.

APRIL 3: Caught a flounder by the bridge yesterday. Things are getting ready to run and spring is getting ready to pounce, with blue-and-green days and soft winds. Let me finish my book.

Reading George Orwell, *Down and Out in London and Paris.* Really an admirable man. Caught in the Depression and drifting among the dregs and the bums, taking them all as individuals and calmly, seeing with somber humor why they are as they are. He watches his own hunger and misery and thrashing as though from afar. The only dull thing of his that I've seen so far was *Burmese Days,* and that impression may have come from my mood at the time of reading it.

One of the best books about Spain's Civil War, which I had read while living in that country, is Orwell's *Homage to Catalonia,* an account of his enlistment in the Republican Army, in which he fought well and was seriously wounded, and of his growing disenchantment as he watched the competitive and often bloody squabbling among the factions on that side—Communist, Anarchist, Socialist, and so on—which was a main reason for Franco's ultimate victory. Finally Orwell, a Socialist, was arrested by the Communists, but managed to escape to France.

He has come under some posthumous criticism for inconsistencies in his political views and for fictionalizing accounts of his personal experiences, but I don't think those things matter much. He was a delightful, very strong writer—political, yes, but full of clear perceptions.

APRIL 7, LATE AT NIGHT: Have been reading poetry, mainly Yeats, in an anthology Paula left here yesterday. It restores confidence, somehow. Yeats especially is so superb and yet he had to go through so much to get to where he did, and to stay calm afterward. Seeing that such use of language is possible, I think, is the reason for the reassurance it brings.

A terrific wind outside, blowing rain out of the east. A good night to be inside and think and read. I ran across a phrase somewhere this evening, "the joy of loneliness." It is true, at least sometimes.

APRIL 10: Alex came over very early this morning to wake me, banging on the door with his brass-headed cane from the Madrid Rastro and coming in and shouting jovially, "This is poetic justice!" because some drunken friends of mine had called his house looking for me at 3:30 a.m. and he couldn't get back to sleep afterward.

Who called?

Spring moves in here by jerks and false starts. A wet snowstorm day before yesterday, and today is all blue and warm. Many birds, and in the afternoon I drove over to Town Beach and watched ospreys hovering, beating in that funny hung-up-by-a-string way of theirs, then dropping slanting down onto fish. Swarms of gulls against a red sunset.

Françoise Sagan, *Bonjour Tristesse*. Rather a nasty little tale of too-wise adolescence. An uncharitable thought: An average French writer would gladly pose as having had perverse sexual relations with his/her father or mother if he/she thought it would shock people. An average American ditto would do the same if he/she thought it would make money.

APRIL 11: Am working well, did seven pages yesterday ending after midnight, to page 164 of III. Then triumphantly drank a lot of whiskey and felt too bad this morning to work.

Caught a good flounder in the afternoon by the bridge, picked up some big oysters on the beach, knocked loose from their bed by a northeaster, and ate all that for supper. Spring moves along, though it's cold still and the change is subtle. Fishermen will line up elbow to elbow on the New York trout streams this Saturday. Let them. I may have a go at that later on, though, if only to be able to say to myself that I've fished the Beaverkill.

[It was and perhaps still is a famous Catskill stream, but I never did get to fish its waters.]

APRIL 12: I have finished writing, for better or worse, the first draft of a novel. It needs retyping, and revision is going to be a tremendous factor in its ultimate worth, and all of that comes now.

(Later) The funny kind of numb indifference you feel when you finish something—not at all the exuberance you think you deserve, or maybe you don't deserve it.

I stayed in Sag Harbor for a few weeks longer, retyping the book and working not very hard on its revision and puttering a great deal. Fixed up an old wooden rowboat of Alex's, which leaked almost as badly after my labor as it had before, and used it to go after weakfish in the tidal channel just out in the bay from my house, anchoring there and chumming with grass shrimp and casting a jig or spoon to the fish when they began to feed downtide from the boat. I caught some nice ones, though I wish now that I'd had the sense to use a fly rod on them, which would have given double the pleasure. But at that time I didn't know anyone who cast flies in salt water.

In June I gave up the house, visited a while with Harry Jackson in New York, trouted for a couple of days upstate with an old Marine cohort named Ben Hadley, and stopped a while with my erstwhile landlady Catherine Spencer in Pennsylvania alongside the Delaware River, where she ran an institution called the Brett School, a haven for retarded or disturbed girls of good (i.e., prosperous) background. Because of the easygoing way in which Catherine handled her girls, and the green calm streamside environs, it was a weirdly happy place in a surreal way, and her friend Thomas Wolfe had often come there to wind down. Then I meandered on toward Texas, stopping with the usual friends along the way—Sam and Liz Hynes at Swarthmore, Jim Derryberry and his Mary Jo in his native Nashville—and ended up at home.

The Brooks remained close friends and we stayed in touch. When Jane Cole, who had gone out for a while with Alex's son by an earlier marriage, moved from the East to Dallas as a designer for Neiman Marcus, they had her look me up in Fort Worth, which led to a New York wedding in late 1958, with

Jane and John, 1957

Alex as best man. Later they visited us at our country place in the Texas hills, and Alex came back again alone, two or three years before he died in 1980, with a great untidy memoir that he wanted me to put in order.

This was a rambling sort of document consisting of thirty or forty individual essays on things he remembered and on his thoughts about art and life and a number of other subjects. Much of the material was intriguing, particularly in the parts concerned with his youthful career in the 1920s and '30s, when he had been in on many important things that were happening, such as the early Whitney Studio Club that later became the Whitney Museum. He had been closely acquainted with just about everyone in the East Coast art world of that time, had been a respected figure among them, and had received much recognition for his painting. His achievements had also led him into friendships with a number of writers and film people. One of his best-known paintings, a portrait of the young Katharine Hepburn in a long red dress, was widely reproduced but later stolen from the actress's home by some admirer who was never found, nor was the portrait.

The memoir also contained a good bit of dross, however, and except for a vaguely chronological progression there was very little linkage between the various essays or chapters as they piled up. All were interesting to me because they reflected the thinkings and weaknesses and strengths of the old guy who had written them and whom I loved. I could even appreciate the occasional swatches of his rather far-fetched humor, with a sprinkling of the puns he loved, and didn't mind his decided opinions (Alex was never short of those, and they were always intelligent if often quirky) on matters ranging from the Altamira and Lascaux cave paintings to the French Impressionists and the superiority of Goya and Zurbarán. I found myself less fond of occasional passages in which he resurrected old grudges from thirty or forty years before, and told him so.

But he wanted none of the material changed in gist or structure. What he asked of me was just to get the grammar and expression in order, and nothing more. I kept trying to establish more continuity between the chapters, more of a flow toward overall meaning, but his reaction was always hell no. So we labored on the thing for two or three weeks and got its expression straightened out, had long talks as friends, and Alex went back to Sag Harbor well pleased.

Various publishers to whom he later submitted the memoir liked it, but said it needed heavy editing to make it hold together—"gappy," one editor called it, which had been pretty much my own view—and Alex adamantly refused to consider such changes. After he died, as his designated literary executor I couldn't place it anywhere either, without agreeing to the drastic alterations he had expressly forbidden. I thought about letting some decent editor have his way with it, but finally decided I didn't need an irascible if beloved old Russian ghost to be haunting me and snapping at my butt. So I placed unaltered copies in a couple of university libraries, where the memoir remains available to art historians and scholars.

EIGHT

The End of a Time

(1956–1960)

Ｉ SPENT JULY in Fort Worth, then drove to Mexico to revise the novel, but in my own inimitable fashion thrashed a bit before knuckling down to that task. First I sailfished with Texas friends on the west coast at Mazatlán and San Blas, bluewater charter-boat trolling. We caught a few of the large handsome creatures, but I found it sad to watch their colors fade as they died on board, for there was little catch-and-release in salt water back then, especially in Mexico where the boat captains would sell the fish on shore as meat. Nor was such a team endeavor, aided by the boats' powerful motors, an agreeable kind of angling to me, being too far removed from the personal poking about on rivers and creeks and salt inlets that has always been my favored form of the sport.

One of the captains did pay me the compliment of believing me to be a Spaniard, a mistake nobody across the Atlantic had ever made. He laughed heartily and shook his grizzled head when I insisted I was puro gringo. I thought again about those possible Mexican cousins out of the Cavitt line. . . .

Then I wandered alone for a couple of weeks. Morelia the hometown of my father's former head tailor, Luís Salorio, who was delighted to see me and plied me with wonderful fiery dishes at his house. Mexico City where I looked up Ángel Sánchez, now a young attorney at a bank and sedately married. Tuxpan; the little Mi Ranchito hotel in its green valley; the trouty hacienda at San Miguel Regla; San Miguel de Allende. . . . But I returned finally, for the main haul, to the old, high-ceilinged Hotel Bellamar in Mazatlán, cooled by steady breezes from the bay it overlooked.

The city at that time was not so much a resort as a sleepy seaport, for the modern highway from California had not yet been constructed, and American access from the northeast was via an unfinished road across the mountains from Durango, the unelegant route I had followed when coming down there in the first place. On it you sometimes had to wait for bulldozers to smooth out humps of dirt and push away toppled trees before you could proceed.

Mazatlán felt just right, so I put the Studebaker into a storage yard and left it there the whole time I was in the city, for anywhere I might want to go lay within walking distance. The streets always had the sound of live music somewhere—mariachis, marimbas, or just some semi-mendicant on a street corner, beating on a battered and badly tuned guitar and howling out old corridos detailing war, mayhem, frustrated love, revenge, hangings, and other agreeable matters. I worked hard and effectively at the hotel, stayed away from women, and in the evenings came to know a little group of expatriate Americans at O'Brien's Saloon, run by a tough and sentimental California lady named Lucille, who fed and liquored some of the broker members of the group on tab. Most of them were mining engineers and prospectors, full of schemes to get rich on gold and silver from the western Sierra Madre. Sipping pale clean Mexican rum in their company, I listened to tales of past successes and failures and of ore that would yield a couple of hundred dollars to the ton, if only the Mexican officials—gringo-haters to a man by these accounts—would stay off of your back. One of the younger members had married a Mexican girl to achieve such liberation; he did love her dearly, he told me, but relations with the officials had been a main stimulus.

With euphoria, I finished revision of the book in late September and drove back to Fort Worth, via the new road to Durango that was still adorned with heaps of rocky dirt and bulldozed trees.

I sent the final draft of *A Speckled Horse* to John Schaffner in New York, and in November he sent it back to me with a long, rather horrified letter listing in detail the reasons he disliked it, which was of course a great boost to my ego. I knew the main reason for his reaction and had more or less anticipated it: he was a gentle, cultivated, effeminate man and the book was quite masculine, with hard edges. But his distaste started me thinking about it and reexamining it, and in the end I became dissatisfied with it myself and decided not to submit it anywhere, even though somebody would almost certainly have been willing to publish it. It was that good, containing long stretches of very strong writing. But it still wasn't as good as I had wanted it to be, and I had done all I could with it.

So much for nearly two years of work that had been sporadic, yes, but full of belief in what I was doing. If you add in the months of thinking and note-making that led up to the writing, and the unproductive period of depression that ensued after I gave up the idea of publishing it, God knows how much time was involved. The whole matter threw me into a tailspin and I thought hard about abandoning my writing ambitions, because I viewed the long effort as a dead loss. I was getting along in years, but there was still time to go to medical school, or to study for the doctorate and turn myself into a genuine academic scholar.

That mood did not last overlong, however. My "downs" have seldom seemed to do so, for there are always too many interesting things around to seize and hold my eyes and mind. . . .

I had expected to move along elsewhere sooner or later, but my father came down with an esophageal cancer that required a horrendous operation, so I decided to stick around for however long a time I could be of help to him and my mother. And in the end this sticking around turned out to last forever. The years away from Texas, to my surprise, had accomplished something I had not anticipated or hoped for, allowing me now to return to home grounds and family and social roots and to see them whole, and to live among them without either rebelliousness or chauvinistic pride. They were entirely mine, but were no longer a burden on my consciousness.

It was a true period of homecoming, and I came to see it as such. Besides a great deal of puttering and hunting and fishing, I immersed myself in other old youthful interests concerning natural and human history. I went out on Sunday-morning bird walks with members of the local Audubon chapter, and spent much time in the Southwestern Collection of the old Carnegie library downtown, boning up on the regional background—the frontier and the bitter fighting between Plains Indians and encroaching white settlers, the establishment of ranching empires, the wearing down of the land. I wrote some short stories based on such material, working at the library and in an empty old servants' quarters behind my parents' house.

I was no longer a speckled horse wandering to and fro among the bottomland myrtle trees. I was where I belonged.

A part of my puttering involved repairing and fiberglassing an antiquated, high-ended wooden canoe, in which I floated down part of the Brazos River to the west, low just then from the continuing drouth of the 1950s. Along with my reabsorption in local matters, this scouting expedition led me a few months later, during the wet, drouth-breaking autumn of 1957, into a longer, three-week trip on the same stream, which held many personal memories from youth that I had nearly forgotten until I was on its waters again. My stretch of the Brazos was also threatened at that time by the proposed construction of several reservoirs, which gave urgency to my desire to see it whole and study it while it still existed.

Characteristically, I saw the voyage as subject matter for an

John and The Passenger (Watty) at the start of the Goodbye *trip*

article, and through John Schaffner obtained an advance payment from a magazine to cover expenses. The trip, though
sometimes cold and wet, was a complete pleasure. Except for
occasional contact with the country's people I had the river pretty
much to myself, I and the little dog I took along. The personal
memories, the stories from bygone times, and the birds and other
richnesses of nature were with us all the way. By the time the
float was finished and the article had been written and published, so much fine material was left over that a book began to
write itself.

This was *Goodbye to a River,* and it flowed as certainly as the
Brazos itself. I remember exulting as I worked on it. Its rightness
wiped out my disappointment over the failure of *A Speckled
Horse,* which I could now see as the last, deck-clearing stage of
an apprenticeship lasting more than a decade and experienced
far from home, during which I had slowly developed a degree of
objectivity in regard to who I was and how to handle language.

After those years of trying, I had finally managed to discern some subject matter that was right for me, and, for better or worse, to attain my full voice as a writer. West Texas vowels and diphthongs, those that had embarrassed me on a tape recording in Madrid a couple of years earlier, were still intact in that voice, but I didn't mind them now. They were mine, and so was the book.

During my work on it I was holding down a teaching job at a local university and it slowed the writing not a whit. Nor did marriage, which took place because I couldn't stand the idea of losing my bright and spirited Jane and I was no longer afflicted with the doubts about my future that had so troubled me in Spain.

It was a liberation, *Goodbye to a River.*

Life began to straighten out. After *Goodbye* was published, I had a career in other people's view, the "touchstone" or "status" whose lack the old journal bemoans in one of its more plaintive passages. I also had the college teaching, many interests that were vital at least to me—too many of them most of the time— a beloved and delightful wife and two gifted and affectionate daughters (who both now have their own families and lives and careers), and a few old friends from youth along with a good many others—from college, from the war, from New York, from Europe—who could be reached through letters or the telephone. And I had left restlessness behind me, except of the kind that eternally afflicts most serious writers and painters and other creators, whose work is seldom quite as good as what they had in mind to start with.

One of the friends who phoned me a year or so after Jane's and my marriage was Park Benjamin, sixtyish now, fairly broke still and living in Houston in a small house that Homer Buck and a couple of his other boys had bought for him, retaining the title themselves so that he couldn't cash the place in, as both he and they knew he was quite capable of doing when short of funds. I had sent him a copy of *Goodbye* and he wanted to discuss it, and to discuss other things at length, reminiscing about his own life and about his boys, who were all doing well in their various professions, and asking about my own activities. Then he wanted to speak to Jane, whom he had not met, and with his acute ear for language was elated to hear in her voice the accents of Old New York, the background from which they were both in a sense escapees.

After they had finished talking and had hung up, she turned to me with a somber face and said, "You know, that's the kind of call someone makes when he's getting ready to die."

She had and still has that kind of unsettling insight. Complex, sometimes ridiculous, but always warm and generous Park Benjamin did indeed succumb to massive heart failure not long after that conversation. . . .

Home, after a while, became a patch of rough and rocky country acreage where I have expended much yeoman energy and—I still find this a bit hard to believe—most of the past forty-odd years. My old fascination with land and creatures and natural forces woke up with a vengeance, leading me into the building of a house and barn and corrals and fences, the supervision of herds of cows and goats, and the dozens of other activities that functional rural life entails.

I had the grace to feel a little guilty about all this from time to time, for a puritanical part of my psyche has always regarded time spent away from books and writing as time wasted.

Which has not, however, kept me from wasting lots of it. . . .

Over the years, in mitigation, these experiences on our holding did lead to a couple of additional books, *Hard Scrabble* and *From a Limestone Ledge,* and to a good many essays and articles.

For the writing impulse had never really left me, but instead had grown stronger with my recognition of the sort of material to which my talents, such as they might be, were best suited.

The long-run result—rather sparse because I got started late and have never managed to quit wasting time on these sideline passions—has been a body of work esteemed mainly within my home region, with a blessed sprinkling of appreciators elsewhere. My main books are all still in print and are being read. The kind of writing I have done has never made me rich, or even prosperous as prosperity goes these days. But at this late point that doesn't bother me much, because most of the work still seems to me to say more or less the things I wanted it to say when I wrote it, and says them in my own way.

Through habit, I continued to make entries in the old journal for a few years longer, but have found little in those further passages of much interest even to myself, so have trashed them without transcription or paraphrasing. The record of this later time of life, insofar as I have wanted to preserve it, is in my published work, wherefore I now gladly bid adiós to the fellow I call Young John, who complains and exults and ruminates and worries and wonders and wanders through these pages.

I could wish the backward bastard had been a bit quicker to discern and pursue right directions in his life and his writing, but he wasn't. At any rate, here he is.

More or less.

A NOTE ABOUT THE AUTHOR

John Graves was born in Texas, was raised there (in Fort Worth), was educated there (at Rice), wandered from there (to the Marine Corps, Columbia University, and many far places), and after returning there in the late 1950s wrote *Goodbye to a River* (1960). Over the years Graves has contributed stories and articles to *The Atlantic, Holiday, American Heritage, Esquire, Texas Monthly,* and other magazines. He has written on conservation for the Department of the Interior and for the Sierra Club—in *The Water Hustlers* (1971)—and has taught college English. He lives with his wife on some four hundred acres of rough Texas hill country that he described in *Hard Scrabble* (1974).

A NOTE ON THE TYPE

This book was set in Granjon, a type named in compliment to Robert Granjon but neither a copy of a classic face nor an entirely original creation. George W. Jones drew the basic design for this type from classic sources but deviated from his model so as to profit from the intervening centuries of experience and progress. This type is based primarily on the type used by Claude Garamond (ca. 1480–1561) in his beautiful French books and more closely resembles Garamond's own type than do any of the various modern types that bear his name.

COMPOSED BY NORTH MARKET STREET GRAPHICS,
LANCASTER, PENNSYLVANIA
PRINTED AND BOUND BY R. R. DONNELLEY & SONS,
HARRISONBURG, VIRGINIA
DESIGNED BY ROBERT C. OLSSON